How to Aud
ISO 9001:2015

Also available from ASQ Quality Press:

Integrated Management Systems: QMS, EMS, OHSMS, FSMS Including Aerospace, Service, Semiconductor/Electronics, Automotive, and Food
Chad Kymal, Gregory Gruska, and R. Dan Reid

AS9101D Auditing for Process Performance: Combining Conformance and Effectiveness to Meet Customer Satisfaction
Chad Kymal

The Art of Integrating Strategic Planning, Process Metrics, Risk Mitigation, and Auditing
J. B. Smith

Advanced Quality Auditing: An Auditor's Review of Risk Management, Lean Improvement, and Data Analysis
Lance B. Coleman Sr.

How to Establish a Document Control System for Compliance with ISO 9001:2015, ISO 13485:2016, and FDA Requirements: A Comprehensive Guide to Designing a Process-Based Document Control System
Stephanie L. Skipper

ISO 9001:2015 Explained, Fourth Edition
Charles A. Cianfrani, John E. "Jack" West, and Joseph Tsiakals

ISO 9001:2015 Internal Audits Made Easy, Fourth Edition
Ann W. Phillips

ISO 9001:2015 for Small and Medium-Sized Businesses, Third Edition
Denise Robitaille

The FDA and Worldwide Quality System Requirements Guidebook for Medical Devices, Second Edition
Amiram Daniel and Ed Kimmelman

Implementing ISO/IEC 17025:2005
Bhavan "Bob" Mehta

The Biomedical Quality Auditor Handbook, Second Edition
Biomedical Division and Bruce Haggar, editor

The ASQ Auditing Handbook, Fourth Edition
J.P. Russell, editor

To request a complimentary catalog of ASQ Quality Press publications, call 800-248-1946, or visit our website at http://www.asq.org/quality-press.

How to Audit ISO 9001:2015

A Handbook for Auditors

Chad Kymal

ASQ Quality Press
Milwaukee, Wisconsin

American Society for Quality, Quality Press, Milwaukee 53203
© 2016 by ASQ
All rights reserved. Published 2016
Printed in the United States of America
22 21 20 19 18 17 16   5 4 3 2 1

Library of Congress Cataloging-in-Publication Data

Names: Kymal, Chad, author.
Title: How to audit ISO 9001:2015 : a handbook for auditors / Chad Kymal.
Description: Milwaukee, Wisconsin : ASQ Quality Press, 2016. | Includes index.
Identifiers: LCCN 2016005431 | ISBN 9780873899277 (soft cover : alk. paper)
Subjects: LCSH: ISO 9000 Series Standards. | Quality control—Auditing. |
  Quality assurance—Standards—United States.
Classification: LCC TS156 .K958 2016 | DDC 658.5/620218—dc23
LC record available at http://lccn.loc.gov/2016005431

ISBN 978-0-87389-927-7

No part of this book may be reproduced in any form or by any means, electronic, mechanical, photocopying, recording, or otherwise, without the prior written permission of the publisher.

Publisher: Seiche Sanders
Acquisitions Editor: Matt T. Meinholz
Managing Editor: Paul Daniel O'Mara
Production Administrator: Randall Benson

ASQ Mission: The American Society for Quality advances individual, organizational, and community excellence worldwide through learning, quality improvement, and knowledge exchange.

Attention Bookstores, Wholesalers, Schools, and Corporations: ASQ Quality Press books, video, audio, and software are available at quantity discounts with bulk purchases for business, educational, or instructional use. For information, please contact ASQ Quality Press at 800-248-1946, or write to ASQ Quality Press, P.O. Box 3005, Milwaukee, WI 53201-3005.

To place orders or to request ASQ membership information, call 800-248-1946. Visit our website at http://www.asq.org/quality-press.

 Printed on acid-free paper

Quality Press
600 N. Plankinton Ave.
Milwaukee, WI 53203-2914
E-mail: authors@asq.org
The Global Voice of Quality®

Table of Contents

List of Figures and Tables .... *ix*
Preface .... *xiii*

Chapter 1 Introduction to ISO 9001:2015 .... **1**
  History of the ISO 9001 Standards 1
  The Quality Management System and Its Processes 2
    QMS Structure and Model 2
    QMS Processes 3
  Requirements of ISO 9001:2015—Becoming Process Focused 4
  Context, Interested Party Expectations, and Objectives. 6
  Planning and Risk/Opportunities. 7
    Understanding Risk 7
    Use of Risk and Opportunities in ISO 9001:2015 8
  ISO 9001:2015 Requirements for Risk. 9
    QMS Processes and Planning (Clauses 4.4.1 and 6.1) 9
    QMS Processes and Planning Risk (Reference Clauses 4.1 and 6.1) 9
    Product and Process Risk and Opportunities (Reference Clause 5.1.2) 9
  Summary of ISO 9001:2015 Requirements for Risks and Opportunities
    and Risk-Based Thinking. 10
  Risk-Based Thinking 11
  What the Standard Does Not Require 11
  What Organizations Need to Do and Auditors Need to Do in Regard to Risk
    and Risk-Based Thinking. 12
  ISO 9001:2015 and the High Level Structure (HLS). 12
  Changes to ISO 9001:2015. 14
    ISO 9001:2015, Annex A 16

Chapter 2 Auditing Strategy for ISO 9001:2015 17
Conformance and Performance Audits 17
Stage 1 Audit—Document Review or a Documented Information Review and
  Audit Planning 17
Stage 2 Audit—Conducting the Audit 18
Audit Trails for ISO 9001:2015—Audit Approach 22
  Overall QMS Performance 31
  Process Performance 31
Conducting a Process Performance Audit 31
  Completing the Process Analysis Worksheet 31

Chapter 3 Conducting the Stage 1 Audit for ISO 9001:2015 35
Documented Information Review 36
Process Approach 37
Sequence and Interaction of the Processes 37
Process Linkages or Process Interfaces 39
Clause- or Function-Based Process Maps 40
A. Documented Information Review 41
  Process Documentation 42
B. Performance Analysis 44
  Customer Scorecards 44
  Customer Complaints and Problem-Solving Efforts 46
  Intended Results and Customer Satisfaction 46
  Evaluate Internal Audits and System Audit Results 46
  Process Approach versus Clause or Elemental Approach 47
  QMS Performance 47
  Measuring Key Indicators and Performance Trends 49
  Identify Suspect Processes 50
C. Create an Audit Plan 51
D. Determine the Audit Feasibility 53
E. Prepare and Deliver the Stage 1 Audit Report 54
F. Update Process Analysis Worksheet or Audit Checklist 54

Chapter 4 Stage 2: On-Site Audit 57
Audit Procedure 57
  A. Conduct Audit of Remote Supporting Functions 59
  B. Opening Meeting 59
  C. Conducting the Audit 60
  C.1 Conduct Facility Tour, If Needed 64
  C.2 Study Customer and Organizational Performance 67
  C.3 Meeting with Top Management 67
  C.4 Audit Organizational Processes 68
  C.5 Verify That All Processes and Clauses Are Audited 69

D. Write Up Nonconformities	69
E. Closing Meeting	73
E.1 Determine Audit Team Recommendations	73
E.2 Prepare the Draft Report	73
E.3 Conduct the Closing Meeting	74
F. Audit Report	74
G. Corrective Action and Closeouts	76
G.1 Evaluate Root Cause Analysis and Systemic Corrective Action	78
G.2 Complete a Follow-Up Audit as Needed	80
Conclusion	81
Appendix A **Introduction to Process Focus**	**83**
Appendix B **Assessment Report for Stage 1**	**91**
Appendix C **Confidential Assessment Report for Stage 2**	**113**
Appendix D **ISO 9001:2015 Conformance Checklist**	**135**
Index	*137*

List of Figures and Tables

Figure P.1	Evolution of quality.	xiii
Figure 1.1	Quality management system.	2
Figure 1.2	Plan–do–check–act cycle in ISO 9001:2015.	3
Figure 1.3	Schematic representation of the elements of a single process.	4
Figure 1.4	Process map showing sequence and interactions.	5
Figure 1.5	Quality management system with context.	7
Table 1.1	Risk and opportunities in ISO 9001:2015.	8
Figure 1.6	Risk in planning.	9
Figure 1.7	Product or process risk.	10
Table 1.2	Major differences in terminology between ISO 9001:2008 and ISO 9001:2015.	16
Figure 2.1	Risk and opportunity audit trail.	19
Figure 2.2	Planning, performance evaluation, and improvement audit trail.	20
Figure 2.3	New product development audit trail.	21
Figure 2.4	Production and service provision audit trail.	21
Figure 2.5	Risk audit trail.	22
Figure 2.6	Risk sampling sheet.	23
Figure 2.7	Planning, performance evaluation, and improvement audit trail.	24
Figure 2.8	Quality objectives sampling sheet.	25

Figure 2.9	New product development audit trail.	27
Figure 2.10	Production and service provision audit trail.	28
Figure 2.11	Turtle diagram.	32
Figure 2.12	Process analysis worksheet.	33
Figure 3.1	Stage 1 audit plan.	36
Figure 3.2	Typical structure of ISO documentation.	37
Figure 3.3	Process map example.	38
Figure 3.4	Clause or elemental process map.	39
Figure 3.5	Functional process map.	41
Figure 3.6	Schematic representation of the elements of a single process.	43
Figure 3.7	Information from customer scorecard.	45
Figure 3.8	Assessment planning table.	45
Figure 3.9	Risk sampling sheet.	48
Figure 3.10	Quality objectives sampling sheet.	48
Figure 3.11	Planning, performance evaluation, and improvement audit trail.	50
Figure 3.12	Stage 2 audit plan.	51
Figure 3.13	Stage 1—nonconformities.	53
Figure 3.14	Process analysis worksheet.	55
Figure 4.1	Stage 2 flow diagram.	58
Figure 4.2	Opening meeting checklist.	61
Figure 4.3	Turtle diagram—example of management review.	64
Figure 4.4	Process map example.	65
Figure 4.5	Process analysis worksheet.	66
Figure 4.6	Risk sampling sheet.	70
Figure 4.7	Quality objectives sampling sheet.	70
Figure 4.8	Sample evidence of corrective action closeout.	77
Figure 4.9	Root cause/problem relationship.	78
Figure 4.10	What makes a great internal auditor?	82
Figure A.1	Process map example.	84

Figure A.2	Turtle diagram.	85
Figure A.3	Organization of processes by location.	88
Figure A.4	Elemental approach.	90
Figure A.5	Functional approach.	90
Figure B.1	Audit plan—stage 1.	93
Figure B.2	Opening and closing meetings checklist.	94
Figure B.3	Classifications of processes.	96
Figure B.4	Documentation and process cross-reference for ISO 9001:2015.	97
Figure B.5	Information from customer scorecard.	101
Figure B.6	Assessment planning table.	101
Figure B.7	Risk sampling sheet.	102
Figure B.8	Stage 2 audit plan.	108
Figure B.9	Stage 1—nonconformities.	110
Figure B.10	Process analysis worksheet.	112
Figure C.1	Confidential assessment report for stage 2.	113
Figure C.2	Opportunities for improvement.	116
Figure C.3	Employee shift details—site/remote/support location.	118
Figure C.4	Risk sampling sheet.	123
Figure C.5	Quality objectives sampling sheet.	123
Figure C.6	Documentation and process cross-reference for ISO 9001:2015.	124
Figure C.7	Stage 2 audit plan.	127
Figure C.8	Process analysis worksheet.	128
Figure C.9	Corrective action request.	130
Figure C.10	Nonconformity chart.	131
Figure D.1	ISO 9001:2015 conformance checklist.	136

Preface

It is hard to believe that I am writing the third update to *How to Audit ISO 9001:2000*, first written in 2001. Much has changed since 2001 when the ISO 9001:2000 standard was first released, and since 2008 when it was subsequently reissued. In the last update to the book, I mentioned that there are two types of auditing: *conformance* and *performance* auditing.

The two different types of audit strategies can be incorporated into one audit methodology. This book will attempt to integrate both the performance audit and conformance audit into one *process approach* audit. This is especially fitting considering that the purpose of risk analysis and planning is to ensure that the *quality management system* (QMS) achieves its "intended results." Additionally, the new standard has a strong focus on process performance that is mentioned in multiple places within the standard.

Quality is changing over time. Quality was thought of as "inspection" over 100 years ago, and has slowly evolved from *inspection* to *quality assurance* to *design* to *business strategy*. The ISO 9001 standard is following the evolution of quality (see Figure P.1) that first started as "product quality" and that over time has come to be defined as "customer satisfaction" and/or as meeting the

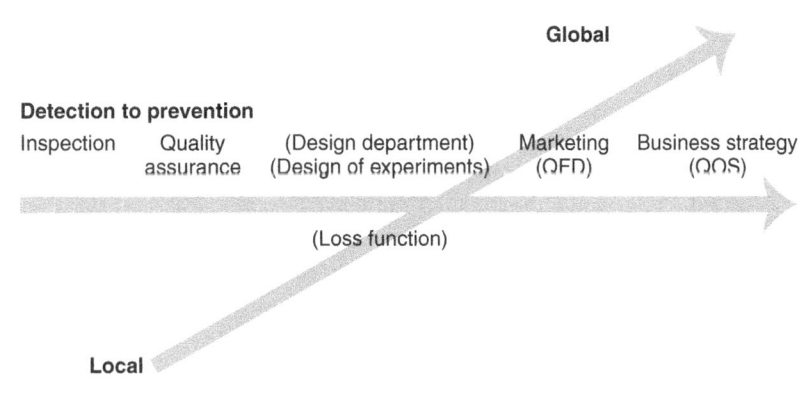

Figure P.1 Evolution of quality.

"needs and expectations of interested parties." It is interesting to note that the word "management" in quality management is defined as *activities to direct or control an organization*. In the note, they mention that *management* includes policies, objectives, and processes to achieve these objectives.

For the first time, ISO 9001 is embracing risk, which is being defined as the "effect of uncertainty" in the organization. If processes help meet objectives (definition of management) then risk analysis is conducted on the processes to ensure that objectives are met. The interaction of the "context"—a new term in ISO 9001—business processes, objectives, goals, and leadership, will lead to some interesting auditing opportunities.

Reflecting on our society, global conflicts, and the fast-paced nature of the world, it is not surprising that businesses are increasingly embracing risk as an important topic in order to safeguard the net worth of the company. There are many areas fraught with product risk due to newer technologies (process and product), intellectual property (IP) risk due to Internet security, international supply chains, new diseases, and wars, and reputation risk due to many factors (social responsibility, quality, scandals, other). Typically, standards reflect business needs.

Integrated management systems remains an important topic, and companies will adopt it because of the savings it represents. This year, I published a book on integrated management systems along with Gregory Gruska and Dan Reid. It is one part of a three part-series that is available or will be available soon from ASQ Quality Press. Books two and three will be on auditing and implementing integrated management systems. I encourage readers to read up on and understand integrated management systems. Be a leader in your organization regarding this important concept.

Another important movement is *sustainability and corporate responsibility*. This movement has not been fully incorporated into management systems. The specialists involved in this movement don't use the same terminology or language as those of us in management systems. However, it is an important movement, and I encourage readers to study ISO 26000 and also the standards and codes of the UN Global Compact, OECD Guidelines for Multinational Enterprises, UN Guiding Principles on Business and Human Rights, Dow Jones Sustainability Index, and the Global Reporting Initiative (GRI). Omnex has added a number of courses in these important subjects, and I see this as a topic that I will write more about in the future.

Chad Kymal
CTO and Founder, Omnex Inc.
Ann Arbor, Michigan

1
Introduction to ISO 9001:2015

HISTORY OF THE ISO 9001 STANDARDS

ISO 9001 was initiated in 1987 with a primary focus on manufacturing. There were 20 requirements, or clauses, each stand-alone, and it covered not only manufacturing, but also included requirements for purchasing, sales (contract review), and design. The 1994 revision of the standard was primarily just a continuation of the ISO 9001:1987 version of the standard, and the changes were incremental.

In 2000, the standard made a radical change and became more of the standard it is today, that is, customer focused and process focused. Along with the customer and process orientation, the standard included requirements for customer satisfaction and continual improvement. In 2008, the standard underwent another mostly incremental change. While there were some significant changes, the authors of the standard (ISO/TC 176) explained that the majority of the changes were merely clarifications and interpretations of the original 2000 revision.

In 2015, the standard is undergoing another radical change. "Radical change" is actually a misnomer. It has added *business context*, and incorporated not only customer expectations in setting objectives, but interested party expectations as well. Most importantly, it has taken on the concept of *risk*, which it defines as "effect of uncertainty."

The second major change in the 2015 revision is the reorganization of the standard into what ISO calls its *high level structure* (HLS) This HLS change, which altered the overall structure of ISO 9001:2015 and of all ISO's *management system standards* (MSS), will be covered in this chapter.

Not only the structure of the standard has changed, but also its internal relationships in terms of the plan–do–check–act cycle, which will also be covered. This is a conceptual change from the old process model, incorporating context, interested party expectations, and risk. Most importantly, it has leadership in the center ensuring that the PDCA cycle is working (see Figure 1.2).

All other sections of the standards are clarifications and enhancements that make this process-focused and interested party expectations–focused standard more effective and efficient (more on the changes in this chapter and in Appendix B).

THE QUALITY MANAGEMENT SYSTEM AND ITS PROCESSES

Let us start with the definition of quality management since this is the intent of ISO 9001:2015. *Quality management* is defined as the policies, objectives, and processes necessary to achieve the organization's objectives as they relate to quality, while *quality* is defined as the degree to which a set of inherent characteristics of an entity satisfies needs and expectations.

In other words, a QMS has a quality policy, quality objectives, and processes (to satisfy the objectives) that fulfill interested party needs and expectations (see Figure 1.1). Interested party needs and expectations will include quality, environmental, health/safety, product, sustainability, and/or any other expectation an interested party may have. However, the focus of the QMS will be in the domain of "quality."

As per the definition of the QMS, the quality policy is related to meeting the needs and expectations of interested parties, hence the arrow from interested party expectations to the quality policy. Also, quality objectives relate to needs and expectations of interested parties, hence the arrow from interested party expectations to quality objectives.

QMS Structure and Model

The ISO 9001 process model from the 2000 and 2008 standards has been replaced with the PDCA cycle used in the ISO 14001 *Environmental management systems* and OHSAS 18001 *Occupational Health and Safety Management Systems* standards. It is a big structural change in the ISO 9001

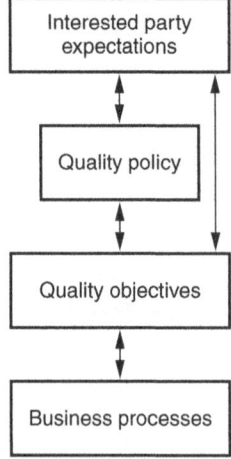

Figure 1.1 Quality management system.

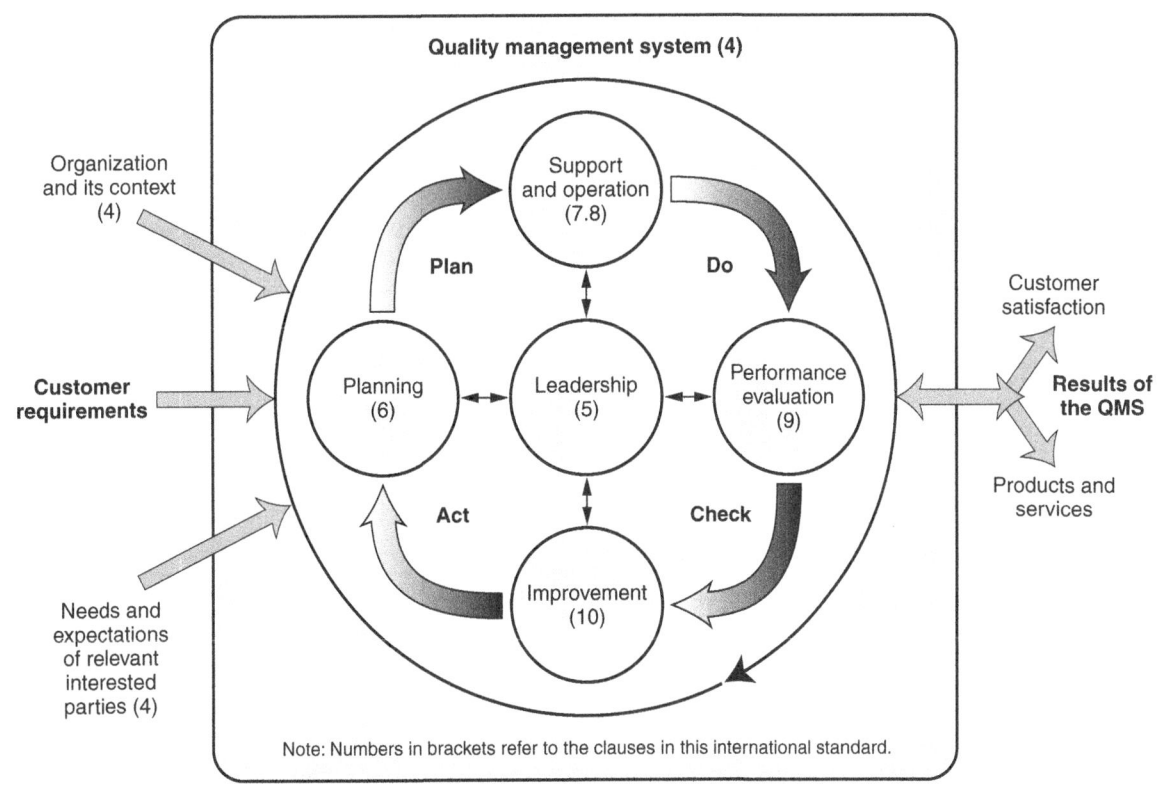

Figure 1.2 Plan–do–check–act cycle in ISO 9001:2015.

standard, with a complete reordering of clauses. The PDCA structure depicted in Figure 1.2 shows three inputs into the planning process, including customer requirements, context, and interested party expectations. The *plan* step includes the process approach (map) and processes, the plan with the actions for mitigating risk, and the quality objectives with the plan to achieve them. The plan gets resourced in terms of manpower, competence, infrastructure, environment, and documented information (documents and records), and then implemented in the *operation,* or do, step, which includes purchasing, new product development, and operations (manufacturing/service). In the next step (check) it gets measured via customer satisfaction, internal audit, and management review. The output from the check step results in actions that need to be implemented for improvement (act).

QMS Processes

The organizational processes required to satisfy ISO 9001 and the requirements of interested parties, and their sequence and interaction, need to be identified. The organization needs to identify the inputs, outputs, criteria, methods, measurements and performance indicators, resources, and responsibilities, as shown in Figure 1.3. Most importantly, in the non-normative section of the standard, ISO 9001 has brought in the idea of risk as it relates to processes by indicating that the controls need to be set based on the risk of each process.

Chapter One

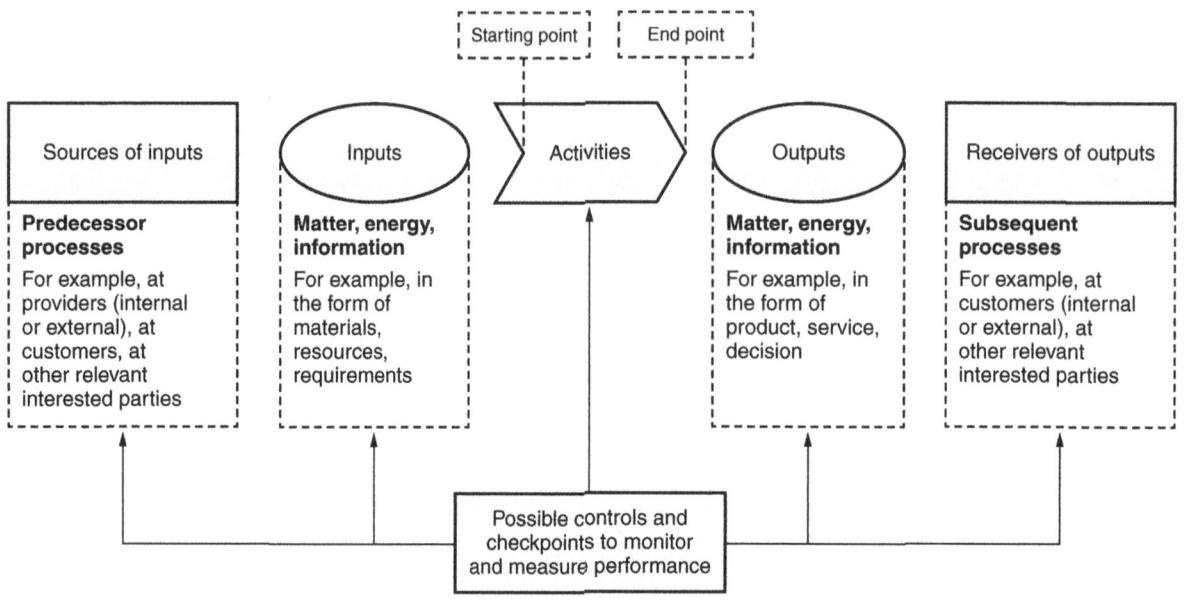

Figure 1.3 Schematic representation of the elements of a single process.

ISO 9001:2015, in regard to the QMS processes, in clause 4.4.1f suggests that risk and opportunities need to be considered as they relate to planning (clause 6.1). In other words, processes need to be considered based on the support they provide the QMS in "achieving intended results."

REQUIREMENTS OF ISO 9001:2015— BECOMING PROCESS FOCUSED

The organization needs to establish a QMS with its processes, including their sequence and interactions. Most organizations satisfy this requirement by means of a process map such as the example shown in Figure 1.4. Auditing the process map is not straightforward. The auditing portion of the book will try to shed some light on the topic of auditing the process focus.

ISO 9001:2015 clause 4.4.1 goes on further to explicitly ask for the following of each of the processes:

a. Inputs and outputs.

b. Criteria and methods (monitoring, measuring, and performance indicators)—some measures could be for control and others could be for process performance.

c. Responsibilities and authorities (who does what).

d. Risks and opportunities as they relate to planning (clause 6.1).

e. Evaluate and make changes to meet process goals and objectives—"intended results."

f. Improve the processes and the QMS.

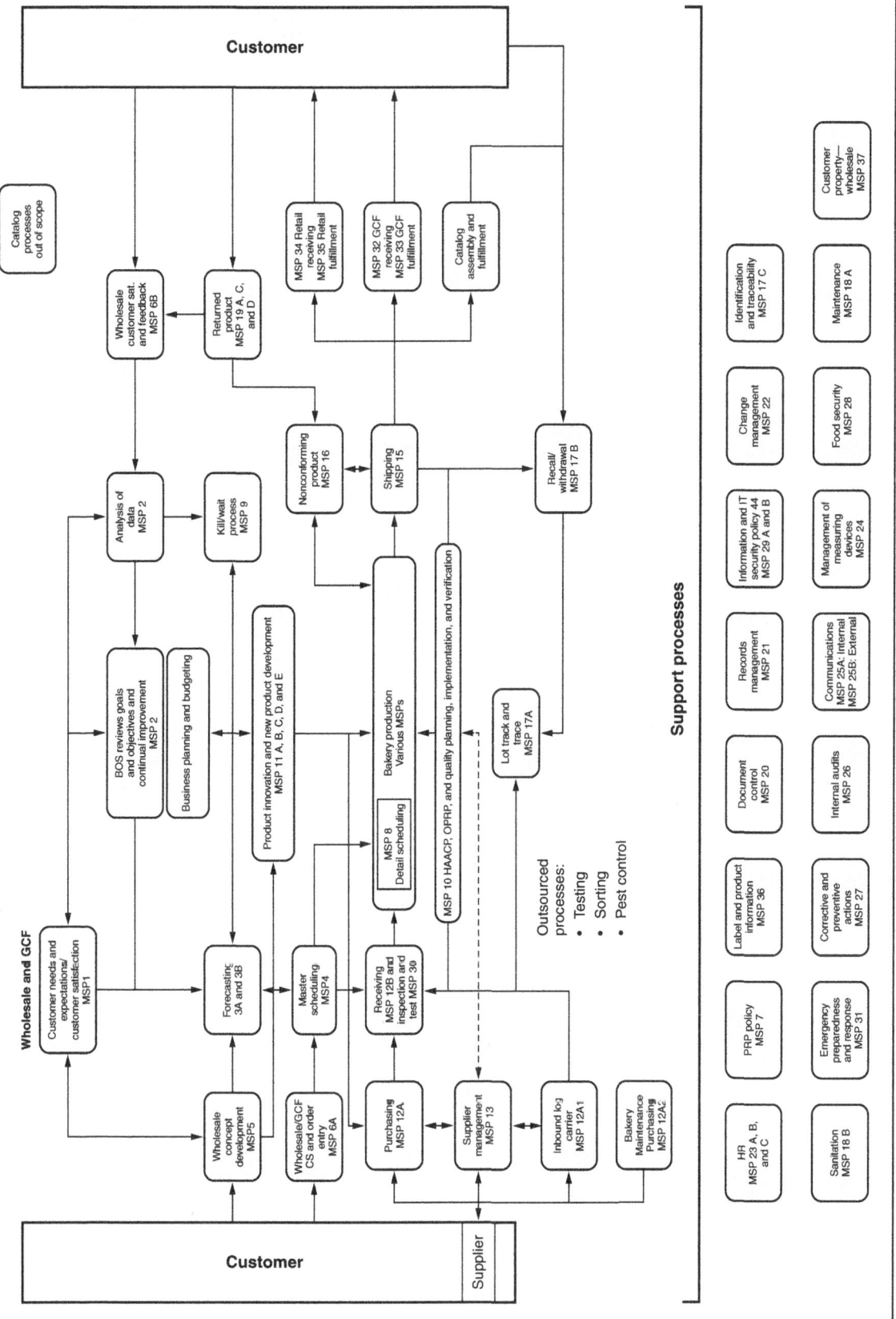

Figure 1.4 Process map showing sequence and interactions.

6 Chapter One

    g. Maintain and retain documented information as required to support processes and to show they are working as intended (read as documentation and records).

    h. Ensure processes are achieving their "intended results" or performing (clause 5.3b).

Some of these explicit responsibilities were not there in the previous standards. Hence, for some ISO 9001–certified organizations, these process-focused requirements could indeed be seen as additional requirements. Specifically, items d, e, g, and h are some of the additional process requirements of ISO 9001:2015.

CONTEXT, INTERESTED PARTY EXPECTATIONS, AND OBJECTIVES

Context is a term that has been hot in business circles over the last few years. Context, or *contextual intelligence*, has been associated with setting company strategy. The argument has been that companies need to consider the context of the organization when they design their strategy and goals and objectives. Dr. Tarun Khanna of Harvard Business School, in a September 2014 article titled "Contextual Intelligence," had this to say:

> *Trying to apply management practices uniformly across geographies is a fool's errand, much as we'd like to think otherwise. To be sure, plenty of aspirations enjoy wide if not universal acceptance. Most entrepreneurs and managers agree, for example, that creating value and motivating talent are at the heart of what they do. But once you drill below the homilies, differences quickly emerge over what constitutes value and how to motivate people. That's because conditions differ enormously from place to place, in ways that aren't easy to codify—conditions not just of economic development but of institutional character, physical geography, educational norms, language, and culture. . . .*
>
> *Context matters. This is not news to social scientists, or indeed to my colleagues who study leadership, but we have paid it insufficient attention in the field of management. There is nothing wrong with the analytic tools we have at our disposal, but their application requires careful thought. It requires contextual intelligence: the ability to understand the limits of our knowledge and to adapt that knowledge to an environment different from the one in which it was developed.*

Context, then, has entered into our lexicon from a business perspective. In short, the context, both internal and external, of an organization will influence the policy, objectives, and processes of the QMS. ISO 9001 says that an organization needs to identify the internal and external issues "relevant to the purpose and the strategic direction and that affect its ability to achieve the intended result(s)." In a note, ISO 9001:2015 suggests that both internal and external issues have to be developed when determining the context of the organization. The external context needs to consider issues from legal, technological, competitive, market, cultural, social, and economic environments, whether international, national, regional, or local. Internal context needs to consider issues related to values, culture, knowledge, and performance.

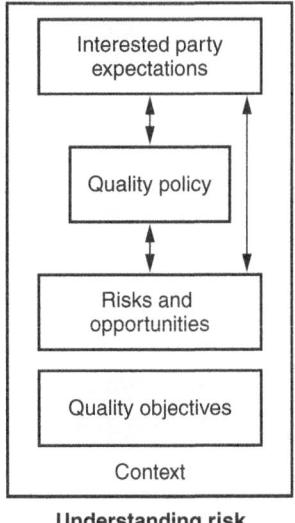

Figure 1.5 Quality management system with context.

The organization then identifies not only customer expectations, but also interested party expectations. ISO 9001 scopes the interested parties and requirements of interested parties to those that are relevant to the quality management system. Once the issues related to the context and the interested party expectations and requirements are identified, what next for the organization?

The organization then uses the context and the strategic direction to formulate the quality policy and objectives (clause 5.1.1b). The organization also uses the context and the interested party expectations to determine the risks and opportunities, and subsequently, the actions to address them (clauses 6.1.1 and 6.1.2) (see Figure 1.5). Strategy is defined as planned activities to achieve an objective (clause 3.35), and hence, strategic direction can be thought of as the mission and vision that define the quality policy and objectives.

PLANNING AND RISK/OPPORTUNITIES

Understanding Risk

Risk is defined in ISO 9000 as the "effect of uncertainty." The notes in the definition go on to further describe risk as a "deviation from the expected," either good or bad. Also, it describes risk as an event that lacks information but which can be expressed in terms of a consequence and a likelihood. Lastly, it states that risk is related to potential events, and that risk is typically expressed as a result of the consequence of an event and its likelihood.

Let us take this opportunity to study risk as it is defined in ISO 14001:2015 *Environmental management systems—Requirements with guidance for use* and in ISO 31000:2009 *Risk management—Principles and guidelines*. The definition of risk in ISO 14001 is identical even though it only includes four of the six notes from ISO 9000. However, the definition of risk in ISO

31000 is a little more specific than in ISO 9001 and ISO 14001, and is defined as an "effect of uncertainty on objectives."

This is a good time to emphasize a few aspects of risk. Risk in ISO 9001:2015 and ISO 14001:2015 is general, that is, a concept that can be applied anywhere in an organization. Risk can be described as a potential event that can be expressed in terms of consequence, impact, or severity of the impact, and its related likelihood of occurrence.

In ISO 9001:2015, opportunities go hand in hand with risk. Everywhere risk is mentioned, it is referred to as "risk and opportunities." It does not appear in ISO 9000 in the definitions, but appears in the non-normative part of the standard. Opportunities are expressed as a positive aspect of a situation since uncertainty can have a positive and/or a negative consequence. In some situations, a positive deviation can result in an opportunity. Opportunities can also arise due to organizations seeking new markets, new products, or new customers as their intended results.

Use of Risk and Opportunities in ISO 9001:2015

"Risk and opportunities" appears in the normative parts of ISO 9001 eight times, and "risk-based thinking" appears once. Risk and opportunities and risk-based thinking appear many times more when we study the informative portions of the standard, that is, the beginning sections and appendix of the standard (see Table 1.1).

Table 1.1 Risk and opportunities in ISO 9001:2015.

Clause number	Title	Explanation
4.4.1	No title—4.4—QMS and its processes	QMS process risk and opportunities as they relate to planning
5.1.1	General	Promoting the use of the process approach and risk-based thinking (top management)
5.1.2	Customer focus	Risk and opportunities that can affect conformity of products and services—this then is broad in scope
6.1	Actions to address risk and opportunities	Appears in title
6.1.1	No title	Consider risk and opportunities as they relate to context of the organization and interested party expectations so that the QMS achieves its "intended results"
6.1.2	No title—risk appears twice	Plan actions to address risk and opportunities, including their effectiveness
9.1.3	Analysis and evaluation	Effectiveness of actions taken to address risk and opportunities
9.3.2	Management review Inputs	Effectiveness of actions taken to address risk and opportunities as they relate to planning (clause 6.1)
10.2.1	Nonconformity and corrective action	Update risks and opportunities determined during planning, if necessary

Legend:
- Refers to risk-based thinking
- Refers to risk implementation
- Refers to check and act cycles

The application of risk and opportunities appears in the standard in three places—clauses 4.4, Quality Management System and Its Processes, 6.1, Actions to Address Risks and Opportunities, and 5.1.2, Customer Focus. So, in the parlance of PDCA, the plan and do steps are in three places in the standard; how about the check and act steps? The check and act steps also appear in three places. Specifically, they appear in clauses 9.1.3, Analysis and Evaluation, 9.3.2, Management Review Inputs, and 10.2, Nonconformity and Corrective Action. Risk appears a lot more in the informative part of the standard than in the normative part of the standard.

ISO 9001:2015 REQUIREMENTS FOR RISK

QMS Processes and Planning (Clauses 4.4.1 and 6.1)

Organizations will develop their own processes as to how they use the external and internal issues list in the context along with the requirements of interested parties to develop their risks, opportunities, and plans. An ISO 9001:2015 note suggests different alternatives in how risk can be addressed, including avoiding the risk, taking the risk because of the opportunity, eliminating the risk source, changing the likelihood or occurrence, sharing the risk, or retaining the risk with informed decisions. Opportunities, ISO 9001:2015 suggests in another note, can consist of pursuing new practices, opening new markets, addressing new clients, building partnerships, using new technology, and other desirable and viable possibilities to address the organization's or its customers' needs.

Action plans need to be developed for the risks and opportunities, and they then need to be integrated back into the QMS via the QMS processes. The processes can then be evaluated for risk as it relates back to planning and helping the QMS achieve its "intended result(s)." *Intended results* could refer to product and service conformance, customer satisfaction, improvement, and meeting quality (interested party expectations) objectives. All of these are requirements of the standard.

For example, one could say, "Our interested party (customer) expectation is *on-time delivery* and we have an internal issue with *competency of personnel* and/or *manufacturing process capability*. Based on this, our risks are (1) loss of xyz customer and (2) loss of $xxx in sales, and there is an opportunity such that if we can get our delivery to 98% on time, we could win back customers A and B that we have lost. Secondly, we could try to enter into ABC market, which requires high quality and delivery.

QMS Processes and Planning Risk (Reference Clauses 4.1 and 6.1)

When the requirements of ISO 9001:2015 are studied, the relationships indicated by the standard relating to the processes of the QMS and planning are as shown in Figure 1.6.

Product and Process Risk and Opportunities (Reference Clause 5.1.2)

Risk as it relates to product and process conformance is general and can be quite broad. Usually, these are areas where risk is generally addressed by organizations. The organization can take a

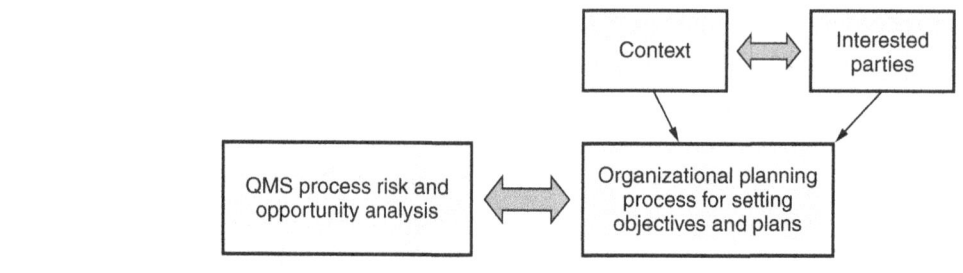

Figure 1.6 Risk in planning.

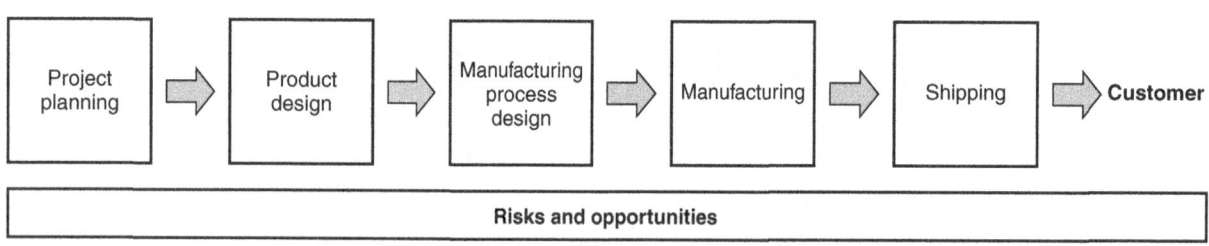

Figure 1.7 Product or process risk.

proactive approach or analytic approach. In the proactive approach, the organization puts in place preventive risk-based systems in project planning, product design, manufacturing process design, manufacturing, and shipping (see Figure 1.7). The alternative is to analyze the product and process conformance (reject) data and identify where the biggest problems are, and then put risk-based systems where they can make the biggest impact.

Omnex's experience has been in the former approach, where project risk analysis, design failure mode and effects analysis (DFMEA) and linked test plans for design risk and process flow, process failure mode and effects analysis (PFMEA), and logistics FMEA were proactively implemented. Data then are used to drive risk, and, hence, rejects are lower time period after time period.

The second part of clause 5.1.2 is about addressing risks and opportunities to enhance customer satisfaction. Focusing on interested parties—and hence customer expectations—and product and process risk will improve customer satisfaction. At the same time, customer satisfaction data (reference clause 9.1.2) should be studied, risk analysis conducted, and improvement actions put in place.

SUMMARY OF ISO 9001:2015 REQUIREMENTS FOR RISKS AND OPPORTUNITIES AND RISK-BASED THINKING

ISO 9001:2015 requires companies to have a process for risk, and the process needs to apply risk-based thinking and address risk and opportunities as they relate to QMS processes (clause 4.1), planning (clause 6.1), and product and process risk (clause 5.2).

- In clause 6.1, risks and opportunities need to be considered in concert with the issues (external and internal) identified in the context, and the requirements of interested parties as they affect the "intended results" of the QMS (read overall business). (Definition: Set of interrelated or interacting elements of an organization to establish policies, objectives and processes to achieve these objectives, ISO 9000:2015 FDIS.)

- Process risk as it affects planning needs to be identified (clause 4.4.1), and the actions identified from risks and opportunities need to be integrated and implemented back into the processes. The effectiveness needs to be evaluated as well (clause 6.1.2).

- The organization needs to address risks and opportunities of those areas in the organization that affect "conformity of products and services (including) . . . enhance customer satisfaction" (clause 5.1.2).

  Note: The organization could consider risks and opportunities in planning that could also include conformity of products and services and enhancing customer satisfaction. The risk strategy is up to each organization.

The effectiveness of risk and opportunities needs to be evaluated by analysis and evaluation (clause 9.1.3), and the effectiveness of the actions associated with the objectives or planning needs to be an input in the management review (clause 9.3.2). Additionally, in clause 10.2.1 the standard requires that risks and opportunities are "updated as a result of a nonconformity."

- The effectiveness of actions taken needs to be evaluated (clause 9.1.3). These actions can come from processes (clause 4.4.1), planning (clause 6.1.2), and/or conformance of products and services and customer satisfaction (clause 5.1.2).

- Effectiveness of actions taken from clause 6.1 and processes (clauses 4.4.1, 6.1.2) need to be covered in the management review.

- Update risks and opportunities determined during planning (clause 10.2.1).

RISK-BASED THINKING

Risk-based thinking appears once in the normative part of the standard as a requirement that top management needs to promote risk-based thinking. Each organization is free to elect their method of promoting it; the auditor's job is to evaluate its effectiveness.

WHAT THE STANDARD DOES NOT REQUIRE

Rightly so, the standard does not prescribe a methodology or require a documented process. It is ultimately up to an organization to choose a suitable generic process or specific methodology to address the above.

WHAT ORGANIZATIONS NEED TO DO AND AUDITORS NEED TO DO IN REGARD TO RISK AND RISK-BASED THINKING

Organizations need to determine their processes for risk-based thinking and risk. How are they planning to address risks and opportunities in planning, for product and service conformance, and enhancing customer satisfaction, and so on, as we described above? The auditor needs to determine whether their response meets the minimum requirements of the standard, and whether it is effective overall.

ISO 9001:2015 AND THE HIGH LEVEL STRUCTURE (HLS)

ISO has developed many different management standards, from environmental to IT standards. The number of standards is only going to continue to grow over time. The lack of a unified structure is a real concern from an alignment viewpoint. The standards are increasingly being implemented as stand-alone silos in an organization rather than one management system. Secondly, it is difficult to understand and translate across multiple systems because of multiple terminologies and structures. The International Organization for Standardization Technical Board understood the need for consistency between the standards and asked the Joint Technical Coordination Group (JTCG) to create a directive for the different management teams. The result is the ISO/IEC Directives, Part 1, Consolidated ISO Supplement, 2013, Annex SL, Appendix 2, which sets out the high-level structure, identical core text, common terms, and core definitions that are to form, when possible, the nucleus of future and revised management system standards (MSS), such as ISO 9001, developed by the JTCG.

- "All MSS (whether they are Type A or Type B MSS) shall, in principle, use consistent structure, common text and terminology so that they are easy to use and compatible with each other.

- The guidance and structure given in Appendix 2 to this Annex SL shall, in principle, also be followed (based on ISO/TMB Resolution 18/2012)."

The HLS of ISO 9001:2015 (and other standards) is shown in the sidebar.

Some thoughts on the HLS for the reader: The HLS does not mean that the organization should structure their procedures as per the HLS structure. The processes should follow the process map of the organization, that is, how the organization operates. Secondly, the HLS allows for easier adoption of an integrated management system. This author published a book in 2015 for the American Society for Quality on integrated management systems (IMS) titled *Integrated Management Systems: QMS, EMS, OHSMS, FSMA Including Aerospace, Service, Semiconductor/Electronics, Automotive, and Food*. This book includes five North American and international case studies in

> **Box 1: Examples from the New Annex SL**
>
> *High level structure:*
>
> - Clause 1—Scope
> - Clause 2—Normative references
> - Clause 3—Terms and definitions
> - Clause 4—Context of the organization
> - Clause 5—Leadership
> - Clause 6—Planning
> - Clause 7—Support
> - Clause 8—Operation
> - Clause 9—Performance evaluation
> - Clause 10—Improvement
>
> *Examples of identical definitions:*
>
> Organization, interested party, policy, objective, competence, conformity.
>
> *Example of identical text:*
>
> Top management shall ensure that the responsibilities and authorities for relevant roles are assigned and communicated within the organization

each of the above-named industries. It is really hoped that with the advent of the HLS, more organizations can take on the IMS strategy.

The process model in ISO 9001:2015 has changed to the structure of PDCA (the plan–do–check–act cycle). Planning (clause 6.0), which we described earlier, considers context, interested party expectations, and customer requirements and goes to the *do* step with Support and Operation (clauses 7.0 and 8.0). Next, it goes to the *check* step for performance evaluation, which includes management review, and then finally to the act step for corrective action and continual improvement.

Top management is in the center of the model, directing the organization and having to show leadership and commitment. There are some interesting requirements worth noting: top management has to take "accountability for the effectiveness of the quality management system," and ensure that the QMS is integrated into the organization's business processes. Overall, it is clear that the standard's intent is that top management is fully engaged in the success of the QMS. Secondly, the QMS must be a part of the core business and is not something only for the quality department. This is a large culture change for many organizations, especially large corporations, where quality organizations and planning/strategy groups are far apart. Since the advent of the ISO 9001:2000 standard, it has been the intent of the standard that the requirements of the standard are for the organization and not just for quality specialists.

CHANGES TO ISO 9001:2015

The changes we have covered so far include context, interested party expectations, risk, process focus, the high level structure, PDCA model, and leadership. The changes in ISO 9001:2015 will be summarized in this section.

- New—4.1 Understanding the Organization and Its Context. Understanding the internal and external factors to identify internal and external issues "relevant to its purpose and strategic direction" and the organization's ability to meet the intended result of the QMS.

- New—4.2 Understanding the Needs and Expectations of Interested Parties. Interested parties are more than just customers, and they are defined as a "person or organization that can affect, or be affected by, or perceive itself to be affected by a decision or activity" (ISO 9000:2015 clause 3.2.3). However, the more interesting section of ISO 9000:2015 is 2.2.4, Fundamental Concepts, which says, "The relevant interested parties are those that provide significant risk to organizational sustainability if their needs and expectations are not met. Organizations define what results are necessary to deliver to those relevant interested parties to reduce that risk."

- Changed—4.3 Scope. Removal of exclusions.

- Changed—4.4 Quality Management System and Its Processes. The standard explicitly asks for inputs and outputs, performance indicators, risks and opportunities, and to evaluate the processes and implement changes to achieve the intended results. It also requires the processes to maintain and retain documented information "to the extent necessary." Another part of the standard requires top management to have someone in the organization ensure the performance of the processes (clause 5.3).

- New—5.1 Leadership and Commitment. Many responsibilities regarding the management system, including ensuring that the QMS is integrated with the business.

- Changed—5.1.2 Customer Focus. Addition of risk and opportunities for product and service conformance and customer satisfaction.

- Changed—5.2—Quality Policy. *Policy* is defined in ISO 9000 as the intentions and direction of an organization, and the *quality policy* as the policy as it relates to quality. The accompanying note expresses it best: ". . . the quality policy is consistent with the overall policy of the organization, can be aligned with the organization's vision and mission and provides a framework for the setting of quality objectives." The quality policy requirements now include these words: "supports its strategic direction." There is also a requirement that it is available to relevant interested parties, which is an increase in scope from the previous version of ISO 9001.

- New—6.1.1 Actions to Address Risks and Opportunities. Planning needs to consider the context (issues) of the organization (clause 4.1) and the interested party expectations (clause 4.2) and address the risks and opportunities to help the QMS achieve "its intended results."

- New—6.1.2 Actions to address risks and opportunities need to be developed and integrated and implemented back into the QMS processes (clause 4.1).

- Changed—6.2 Quality Objectives and Planning to Achieve Them. The planning for the quality objectives (clause 6.2.2) is very explicit.

- Changed—6.3 Planning of Changes. There are multiple requirements on "changes" throughout the standard. Cumulatively, they address "manage the change" which is a new requirement.

- New—7.1.6 Organizational Knowledge. Knowledge necessary for the organization to achieve the organization's objectives.

- New—7.5 Documented Information. Replaces "documents" and "records." Documented information allows freedom in media and format for information in regard to the management system, including evidence of its successful operation, that is, objective evidence.

- Changed—8.1 Operational Planning and Control. No statistical techniques cited in the standard.

- Changed—8.3 Design and Development of Products and Services. Removed Design Verification and Design Validation as specific sub-clauses though they are still required in 8.3.2c.

- Changed—8.4 Control of Externally Provided Processes, Products, and Services. Includes suppliers, a supplier who could be from within your organization (sister plant), and/or outsourced processes.

- Changed—8.5.1 Control of Production and Service Provision. The requirements for production and service to be conducted in a "controlled condition" is explicit and clear in the standard.

- New—8.5.6 Control of Changes. Manage the changes related to production and service provision.

- New—9.1.3 Analysis and Evaluation. Effectiveness of actions on risks and opportunities.

Table 1.2 Major differences in terminology between ISO 9001:2008 and ISO 9001:2015.

ISO 9001:2008	ISO 9001:2015
Products	Products and services
Exclusions	Not used (See Clause A.5 for clarification of applicability)
Management representative	Not used (Similar responsibilities and authorities are assigned but there is no requirement for a single management representative)
Documentation, quality manual, documented procedures, records	Documented information
Work environment	Environment for the operation of processes
Monitoring and measuring equipment	Monitoring and measuring resources
Purchased product	Externally provided products and services
Supplier	External provider

- New—9.3 Management Review. Extend internal issues and effectiveness of actions on risks and opportunities.

- New—10.1 General. Opportunities for improvement for "preventing or reducing undesired effects."

- New—10.2 Nonconformity and Corrective Action. "Update risks and opportunities" based on corrective actions.

ISO 9001:2015, Annex A

There have been terminology changes made from ISO 9001:2008 to the ISO 9001:2015 standard. Table 1.2 (Table A.1 from ISO 9001:2015) summarizes the main changes. The term "product" in ISO 9001:2008 always included services; however, the ISO/TC 176 committee felt a need to specify that products include services by explicitly calling it out in the ISO 9001:2015 revision. This is a continuation of the focus the standard is directing toward the service sector. In a major change, ISO 9001:2015 will no longer refer to *documentation* or *records* but to *documented information*. The words "maintain" will be used to refer to documents, and "retain" for records. Other major changes include terminology changes for purchased product and supplier.

2

Auditing Strategy for ISO 9001:2015

CONFORMANCE AND PERFORMANCE AUDITS

There are two types of audits that can be performed: conformance audits and performance audits. *Conformance* audits confirm that the organization is meeting the requirements of the standard, and *performance* audits confirm that the QMS is achieving its intended results. Performance audits focus on the effectiveness of processes and the quality management system. In this book, performance audits with turtle diagrams and process analysis sheets will be integrated into the conformance audit. In ISO 9001:2015, the raison d'être for the management system is to achieve intended results and for its processes to perform. Performance audits can also be conducted by themselves or in concert with conformance audits. Especially when the system has matured, the organization can move from conformance to performance over time.

Conformance audits require the auditor to conduct a thorough document review of the documented processes. For a system audit, all processes/clauses are sampled to ensure they conform to the documented process and/or ISO 9001:2015 standard. Performance audits focus on whether the system is achieving "intended results" and/or the processes are performing and improving, based on the process measures or checkpoints monitoring them. One could argue that a good conformance audit needs to include performance. However, a performance audit can be conducted without checking for conformance.

STAGE 1 AUDIT—DOCUMENT REVIEW OR A DOCUMENTED INFORMATION REVIEW AND AUDIT PLANNING

When a system is initially implemented, a document review needs to be performed to ensure that the management systems' "documented information" fully complies with the standard. The document review can capture the organization's approach to documentation and records, and the structure of the documented information. The organization's approach to meeting the requirements in clause 4.4.2 is studied in the document review. In other words, what type of documented information does the organization have to support the operation of the processes, and what type of retained information do they have to show that the processes are being carried out as planned?

During document review the general principle is that the organization needs to have processes that meet or satisfy all requirements of ISO 9001:2015. Another general principle is that all processes need (some) evidence that the process is working. Yet another principle includes the idea that processes do not need to be documented. Finally, what documented information is retained is a decision of the organization based on many factors, including size of the organization, competence of personnel, risk of the process, and maturity of the process. Systems are not designed to satisfy the auditor; rather, systems are designed to make the organization successful.

The second part of the stage 1 audit is audit planning. A system audit needs to cover all the processes in an organization and all the clauses of the ISO 9001:2015 standard. The audit plan needs to be process focused and performance based. Both of these topics will be covered in the next section on the stage 2 audit.

STAGE 2 AUDIT—CONDUCTING THE AUDIT

Next, an on-site audit needs to be performed. This audit can be organized around audit trails. Using the process map of the organization, the processes that include the audit trails (groups of processes/clauses) described below can be audited together in the sequences that will be described in this chapter. ISO 9001:2015 will be broken into the following audit trails:

  a. Risk and opportunity

  b. Planning, performance evaluation, and improvement

  c. Leadership

  d. New product development

  e. Production and service provision

  f. Support process

  g. Performance-based audits

The performance audit can be tacked onto the beginning or end of a conformance audit of one process or an audit trail. It also can be done as a stand-alone audit of all relevant processes (more on this later).

One auditor will audit all the processes/clauses in an audit trail. Audit trails have linkages from one area to the next, and the linkages are made with the samples taken.

A. *Risk and opportunity.* This audit trail studies the risk and opportunity evaluation conducted during planning to ensure that the QMS achieves its "intended purpose." The actions identified to

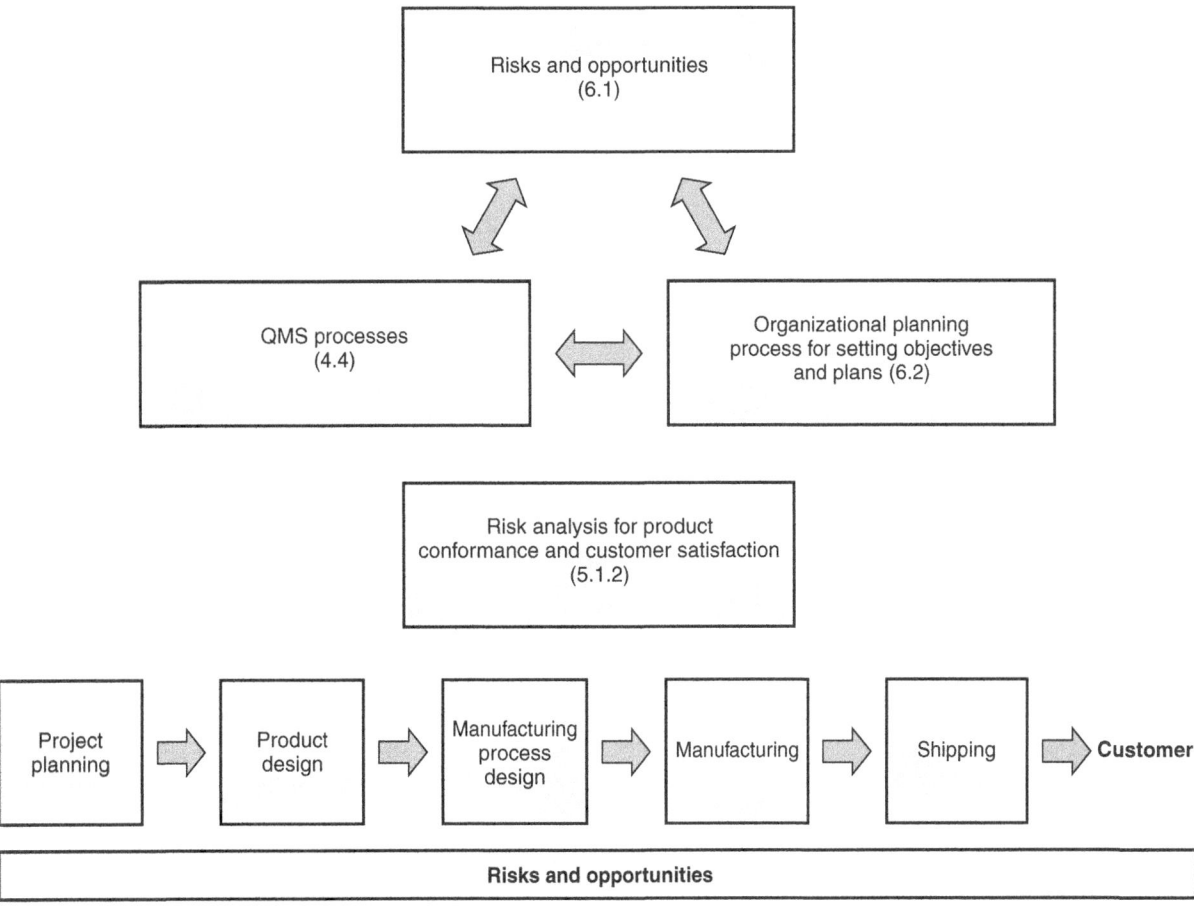

Figure 2.1 Risk and opportunity audit trail.

mitigate the risk (or to take advantage of the opportunity) then need to be integrated back into the QMS processes (see Figure 2.1). Risk evaluation includes studying how risks and opportunities are considered as they affect product and service conformance and customer satisfaction.

B. *Planning, performance evaluation, and improvement audit trail.* This audit trail evaluates the alignment of context, interested party expectations, and policy to the objectives set and whether it is deployed down the organization. It studies the management review for the results of the organization's activities and evaluates whether they are improving and whether the QMS is achieving its intended results. If it is not, the company must make the needed changes (see Figure 2.2).

Since this audit trail has so many important topics and is so large, it is broken into two pieces so that a second auditor is able to audit the bottom half of the audit trail. Risk could have been integrated into the audit trail; however, it is purposely moved into its own audit trail for convenience.

Ideally, the risks and opportunities process should be audited by the auditor who does the second half of the planning audit trail, where analysis, corrective action, and customer satisfaction processes also reside. Each of these processes contributes a piece to risk effectiveness.

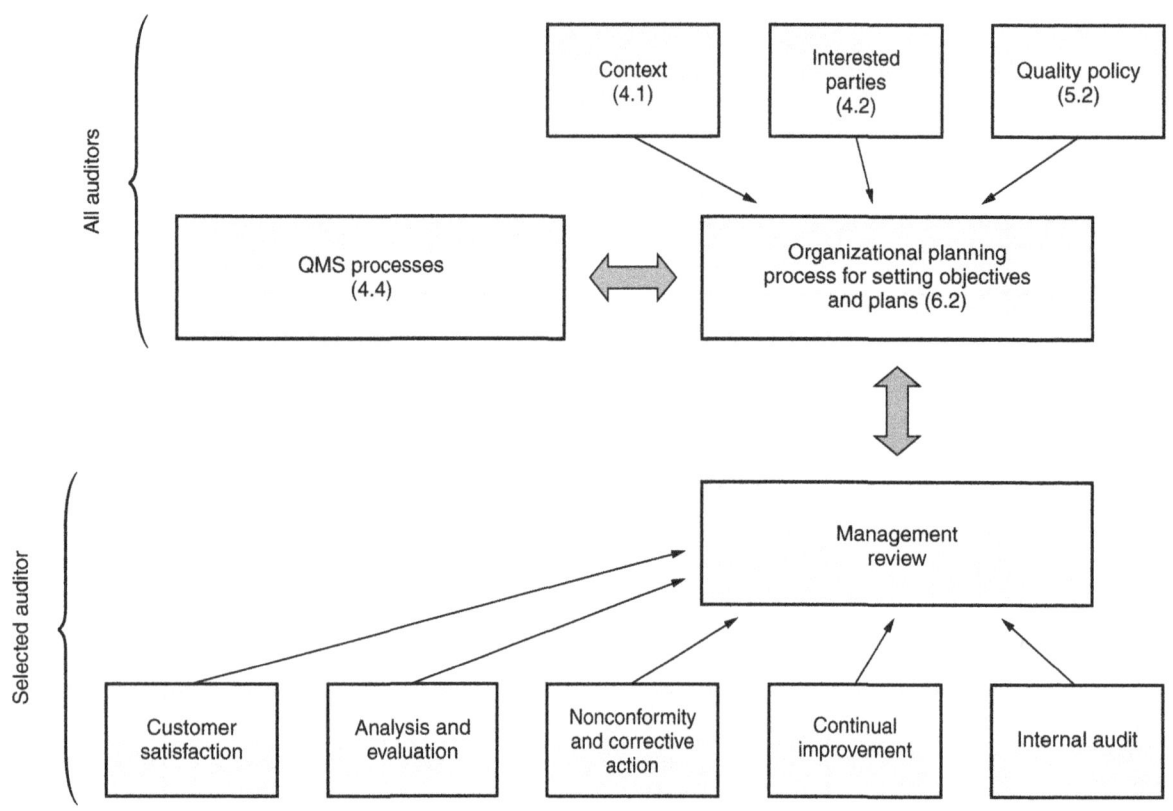

Figure 2.2 Planning, performance evaluation, and improvement audit trail.

C. *Leadership.* This is not really an audit trail other than to interview top management and evaluate their commitment by examining their actions as they relate to the quality management system requirements.

D. *New product development (NPD).* The new product development process starts with the sales process or the contract review process (as it was referred to in the old ISO 9001:1987 standard). Once the contract is won, the organization plans the product design and the manufacturing or production and service provision. It could be one contiguous process; however, to help ease of auditing with different auditors, it has been broken into two pieces (see Figures 2.3 and 2.4).

E. *Production and service provision.* In many organizations new product development is done in one location and production and service provision is done elsewhere. The production and service provision actually provides the product or service to the customer. This is an important audit trail especially because it is a critical process for delivering "good" products and services to the customers.

F. *Support process*:

    a. Resources

    b. People (clauses 7.1.2, 7.2, and 7.3)

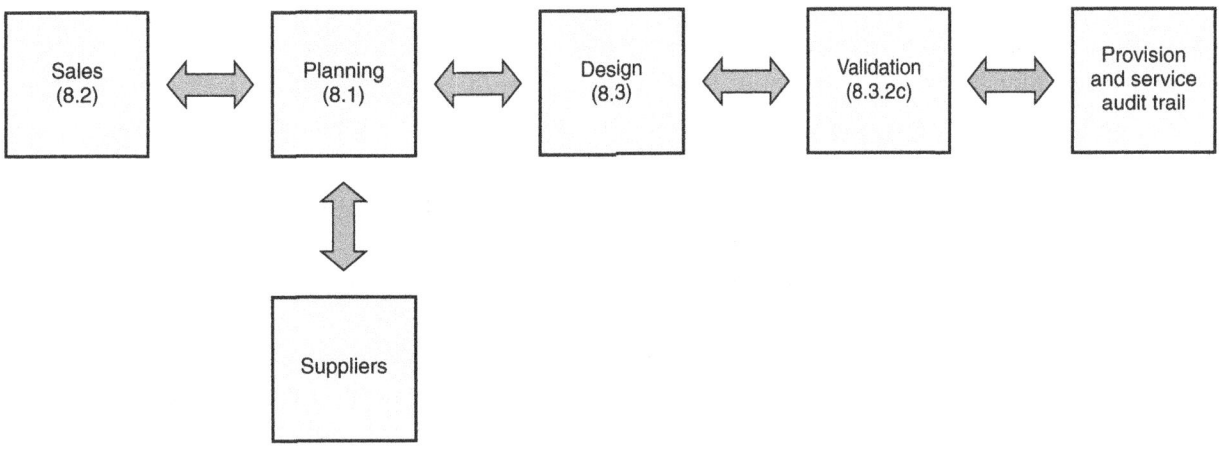

Figure 2.3 New product development audit trail.

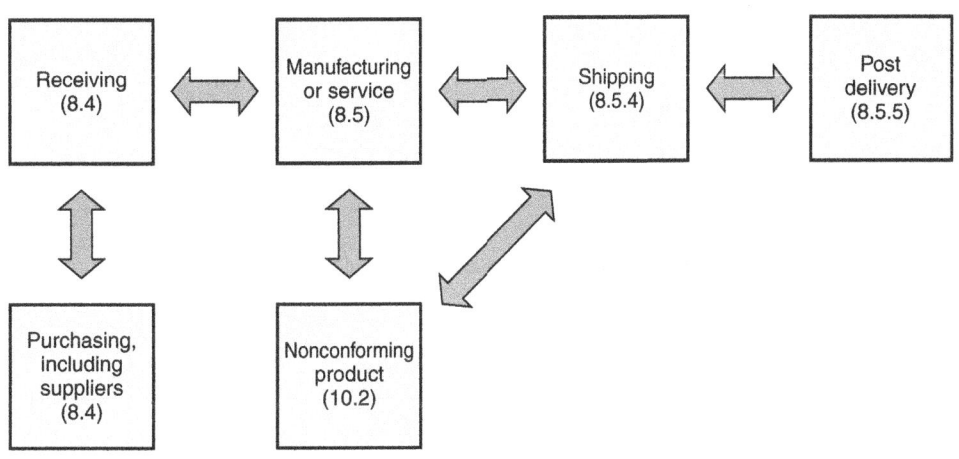

Figure 2.4 Production and service provision audit trail.

c. Infrastructure

d. Environment for the operation of processes

e. Communication

These are support processes that can be audited as they apply throughout the organization and also how they are managed by the process owner. Support processes are enablers that support both the product delegate processes and the management processes in an organization. In most cases, they are not auditable in one location, but are pervasive throughout the organization. The only exception is "resources," which can typically be audited in the HR department. However, training and competency processes that are championed in the HR department need to be audited throughout the company. Processes supporting infrastructure, environment, and communications also need to be audited throughout the organization.

G. *Performance-based audits.* These start with performance-based audit plans in the stage 1 audit. Performance-based audits focus on the process in question and use a turtle diagram that probes competence, resources, inputs, outputs, and measurement/monitoring of the process competence and resources. It asks the question of whether the process measures are aligned with the overall objectives/mission/vision of the organization, and also whether the company is succeeding in meeting their targets and whether they are improving.

The turtle diagram and a process analysis tool will be used in the performance-based audit.

AUDIT TRAILS FOR ISO 9001:2015—AUDIT APPROACH

In this section each of the audit trails will be studied in greater detail.

A. *Risk and opportunity.* Ideally, the risks and opportunities process should be audited by the auditor who does the planning audit trail (see Figure 2.5). This audit trail begins by evaluating

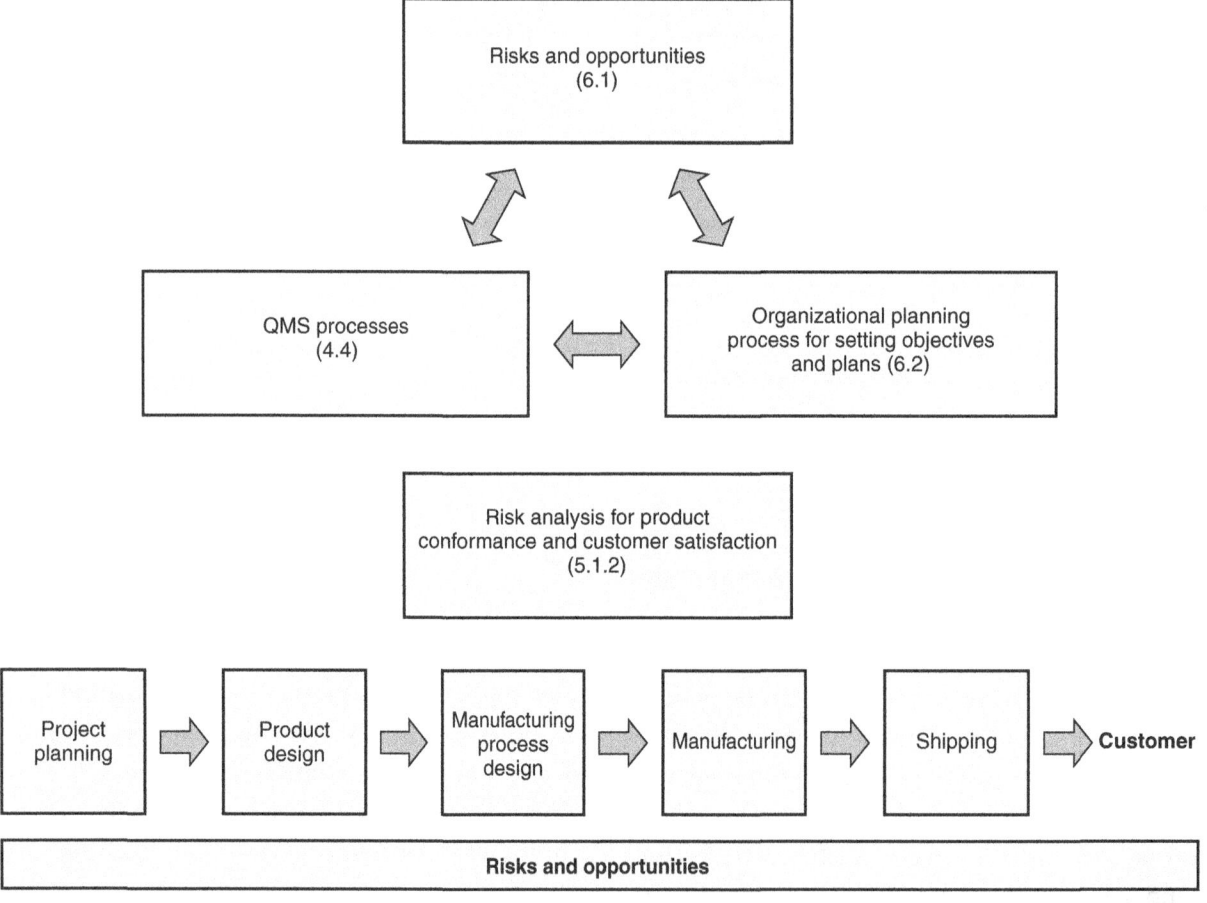

Figure 2.5 Risk audit trail.

the internal and external issues of the organization and the interested parties' expectations. This along with the quality policy determines the "intended results" of the organization. Typically, they are the quality objectives, but the organization needs to determine what they have defined as the "intended results" of the QMS. The organization is then required to address the risks and opportunities to ensure that the organization is able to achieve its intended results or objectives. Use the Risk Sampling Sheet for auditing this audit trail (see Figure 2.6).

The organization needs to analyze data and then determine the "risk and opportunity." Sample three to five objectives and/or "intended results" of the organization. Select the related interested party expectation and internal and external issues as they apply to the objectives and/or "intended results" selected. Document them in the sampling sheet. Next, identify the risks and opportunities that the organization has determined. Does the risk identify the consequence (severity or impact) and frequency of occurrence? What is the plan to address these risks and opportunities? Has the organization integrated these actions into the QMS processes? Is there evidence in the management review that the actions are implemented and that they are effective? Does it appear that the organization has mitigated the risk? "Note 1: Options to address risks can include avoiding risk, taking risk in order to pursue an opportunity, eliminating the risk source, changing the likelihood or consequences, sharing the risk, or retaining risk by informed

Risk Sampling Sheet					
Related interested party expectations* and internal/external issues (4.1 and 4.2)	Objectives and/or intended results (6.1.1)	Related risk and opportunities (6.1.1)	Plan to address risk and opportunities (6.1.2)	Related processes (6.1.2)	Evidence of actions implemented and effectiveness tracked (9.3.2)

*Note: Which internal and external issues and expectations are key to the organization? Has the organization adequately handled these expectations and issues when they set the objectives or "intended results?"

Figure 2.6 Risk sampling sheet.

decision. Note 2: Opportunities can lead to the adoption of new practices, launching new products, opening new markets, addressing new customers, building partnerships, using new technology, and other desirable and viable possibilities to address the organization's or its customers' needs" (ISO 9001:2015, clause 6.1.2).

The second part of the risk audit trail asks whether the organization has determined the risks and opportunities that affect the conformity of products and services. Figure 2.5 suggests that the risks and opportunities can be mitigated in the new product development process starting with project planning, then in product and manufacturing process design, and finally in the manufacturing and delivery process. Risks and opportunities also need to be ascertained in the customer satisfaction process.

B. *Planning, performance evaluation, and improvement.* This audit trail evaluates the alignment of context, interested party expectations, and policy to the organizational objectives, and determines whether it is deployed down the organization (see Figure 2.7). It studies the management review for the results of the organization's activities and evaluates whether the performance results show that they are improving and whether the QMS is achieving its intended results. If they are not, the company must make the needed changes.

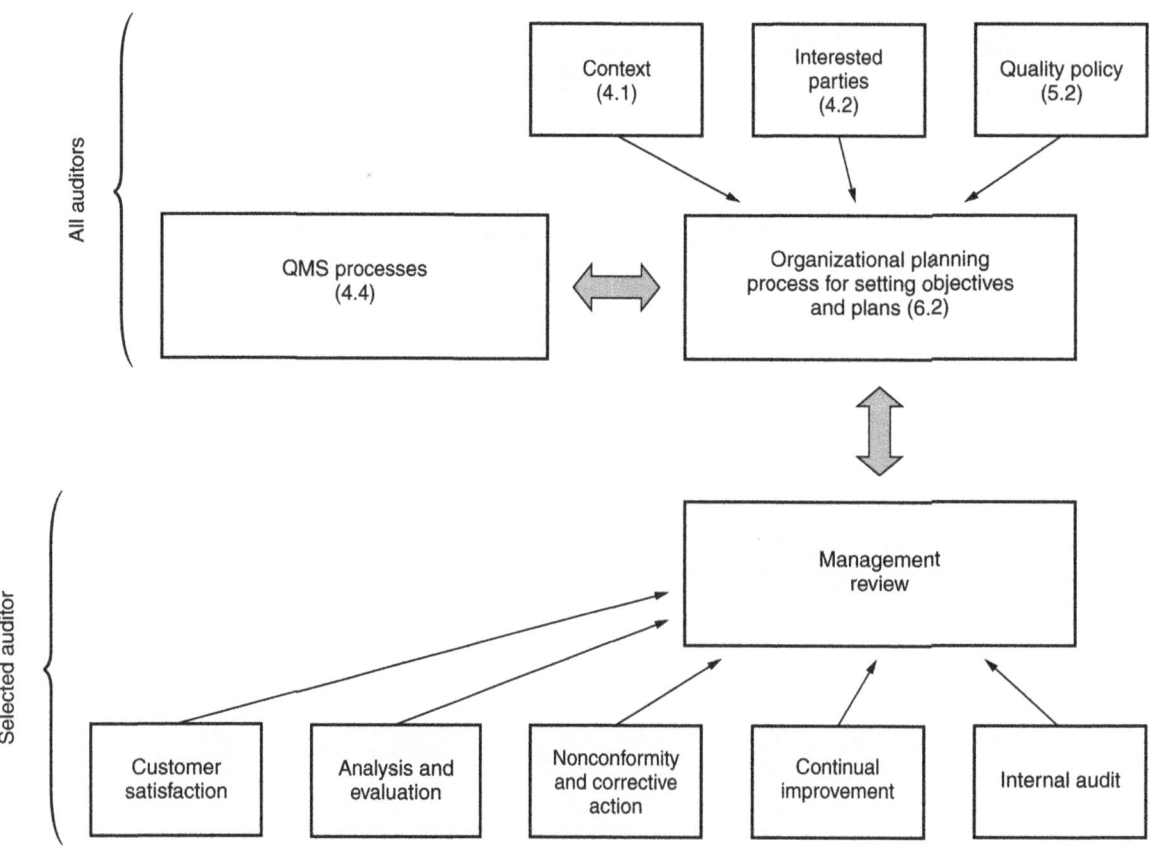

Figure 2.7 Planning, performance evaluation, and improvement audit trail.

Quality Objectives Sampling Sheet				
Quality objectives	Plan for meeting objectives (what will be done, resources, who is responsible, when it will be completed, how results will be evaluated) (6.2.1)	Deployed objectives (sample department and identify deployed objectives)	Objective evidence of objectives being met and actions completed (9.3.2)
*Quality objectives relate to the needs and expectations of interested parties and could result in objectives related to product quality, on-time delivery, or other expectations critical to an interested party, including customers. Note: Clause 6.2.1 requires quality objectives to be consistent with quality policy, be measurable, satisfy requirements, be relevant to products/services and customer satisfaction, and be monitored, communicated, and updated.			

Figure 2.8 Quality objectives sampling sheet.

Since this audit trail has so many important topics and is so large, it is broken into two pieces so that a second auditor is able to audit the bottom half of the audit trail. Risk could have been integrated into the audit trail; however, it is purposely moved into its own audit trail for convenience.

This audit trail picks up where the Risk Sampling Sheet leaves off. The same objectives can be sampled on the Quality Objectives Sampling Sheet (Figure 2.8). The plan for meeting the objectives is documented next, and then in the management/business review the auditor can gather objective evidence on whether the organization has implemented the plan and whether it is showing results, that is, improvement.

The auditor can also sample departments and determine whether the objectives are deployed in the organization. This is also documented in the Quality Objectives Sampling Sheet. My suggestion is to sample three to five objectives.

C. *Leadership.* This is not really an audit trail other than to interview top management and evaluate their commitment by examining their actions as they relate to the quality management system requirements.

In the stage 2 on-site audit, top management will need to be present and answer questions while the planning and risk audit trails are audited. Top management additionally should be interviewed in regard to the following (key words from the standard are shown in *italics*):

- In-depth knowledge of the "planned results" of the QMS and the quality objectives and the status of the actions necessary to achieve them.

- Alignment of the context, interested party expectations, quality policy, objectives, and *compatibility* with the strategic direction of the organization.

- *Integration* of the QMS with the business processes. In other words, there is only one set of processes running the organization.

- Understanding and *promotion* of risk-based thinking and the process approach.

- What the QMS *intended results* are and whether the organization is meeting them.

- Understanding of customer expectations and customer satisfaction and steps taken to improve customer satisfaction.

- Involvement in establishing, implementing, and maintaining the quality policy.

- Understanding of customer and regulatory requirements and whether the organization is in compliance (*consistently met*). How do they track the requirements? What is the process for understanding and meeting them?

- Whether top management is taking ownership of the effectiveness of the management system. Whether they are taking an active role in working with subordinates (*engaging, directing and supporting*) and/or others in ensuring *effectiveness.*

- *Supporting* other managers in performing their responsibilities, that is, *demonstration* of leadership.

- Review of the quality management system at a periodic frequency to assess the "*suitability, adequacy, effectiveness, and alignment*" with the organization's overall "*strategic direction.*"

- Role in assigning specific roles and responsibilities as required (see clause 5.3).

The points above directly relate to clauses 5.0, Leadership, and 9.3, Management Review. Not understanding what the standard means and/or top management delegating responsibilities to others could very well result in a nonconformance for top management.

Overall, do the interactions with top management show a good understanding of the QMS and its performance? Is top management "accountable" to the effectiveness of the QMS?

D. *New product development (NPD).* The new product development process starts with the sales process or the contract review process (as it was referred to in the old ISO 9001:1987 standard). Once the contract is won, the organization plans the product design and the manufacturing or production and service provision (see Figure 2.9). It could be one continuous process; however, to help ease of auditing with different auditors, it has been broken into two pieces, one for new product development and another for manufacturing. (The design and manufacturing may be in different locations.)

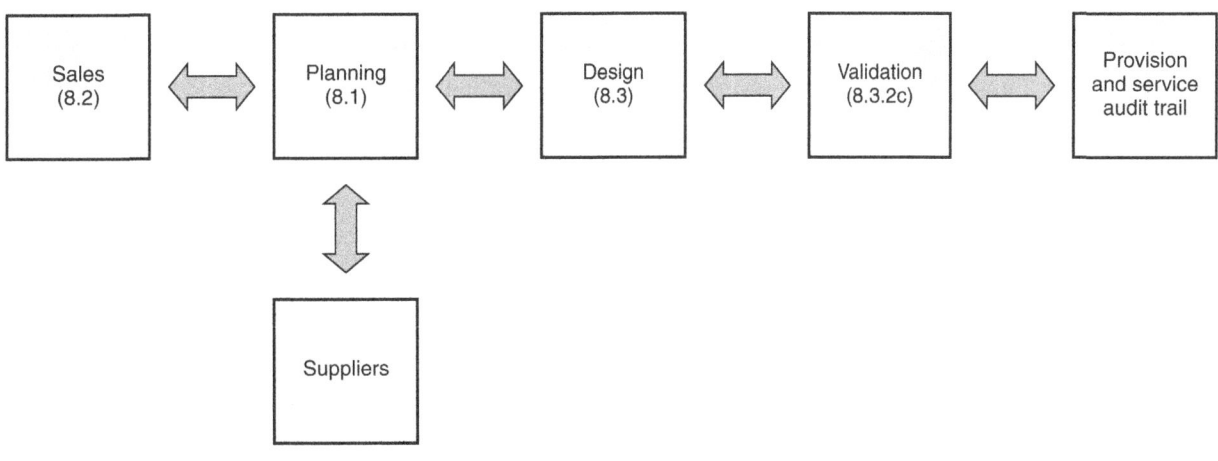

Figure 2.9   New product development audit trail.

The success of the new product development process is vital to the future of the organization being audited. This process is ineffective in many organizations, leading to problems with timing, product quality at launch, and designs that don't meet customer expectations.

The audit trail starts by identifying requirements for the product or service (clause 8.2), then proceeds to program planning or operational planning (clause 8.1), and design and development of the product or service (clause 8.3). In many industries such as aerospace or automotive, there is a first-article inspection (FAI) or production part approval process (PPAP) before the product is released to production or manufacturing. (In some industries, such as semiconductor design, technology and product development occurs first.) After the new product development, the audit moves to the provision audit trail.

Links and samples. The set of links in this audit trail are those from product and service requirement (clause 8.2) through to the product release (PPAP or FAI, for example) to manufacturing. To audit this trail, the auditor first selects product samples and audits the "product requirements gathering and review process" typically conducted before a commitment to supply the product or service is made. This process occurs during the sales cycle, before the proposal is made to the customer. This will verify that the organization has properly identified and reviewed the product or service requirements prior to agreeing to supply the product or service. To ensure that there's a trail to operational planning and then into manufacturing, the auditor will need to identify the products or services that have recently been through the design process and are being manufactured in the plant (also similar in a service environment). If contracts are randomly sampled in sales, they may or may not trail into the manufacturing plant being considered, especially if there are multiple plants in the organization.

Next, the auditor examines how the organization has planned the processes required to produce the product or service identified in Operational Planning and Control (clause 8.1). This audit of operational planning takes place where the organization conducts its project or program management. During this phase, or early in the audit trail, the auditor needs to document the goals and objectives of the product launch. What were the timing, quality goals, and budget at the start of the program? Those in the organization who were involved with program or project management should be able to identify their initial objectives and what the results were for the new product development process.

The auditor then tracks the product or service sampled through design and development (clause 8.3) to test that each step of the new product and process development processes has been followed. Finally, the product approval process (such as PPAP or FAI) is reviewed for content and effectiveness, if applicable.

It's always good to sample a variety of products or services, including those that have been running for one year, were recently introduced, or are still in the pipeline. The auditor should try to audit each of these and others chosen randomly when auditing the requirements gathering and review (clause 8.2). In this way, contracts that were won and lost will be audited. The auditor can study how customer requirements for a particular product or service were gathered by the organization, as required in clause 8.2.

The audit scope and product and service definition are important on this audit trail because a product could include hardware, software, and processed material. The auditor should carefully define the scope ahead of time.

E. *Production and service provision.* The provision audit trail covers all the activities necessary to produce, manufacture, and deliver products and services to the customer (see Figure 2.10). It includes activities for operating the realization processes, identification and traceability of the products and services, handling customer property, preserving product, measuring product and service output, and handling nonconforming product.

The auditor must carefully study the different processes in the organization for production and service provision (clause 8.5) and sample them appropriately. For example, in a manufacturing

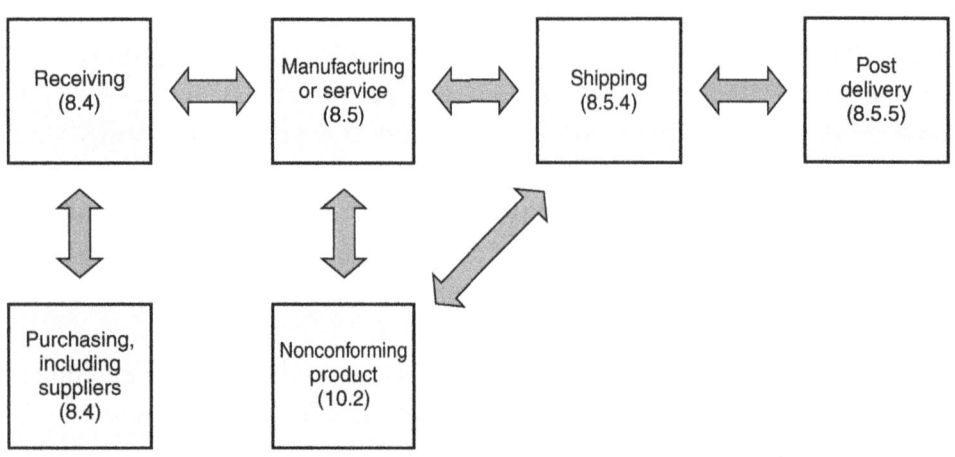

Figure 2.10 Production and service provision audit trail.

plant that performs heat-treating, machining, paint, and assembly, each of these processes should be sampled.

This audit trail starts with receiving inspection or verification (clause 8.4) and production and service provision (clause 8.5), then tracks through all the other processes in operations. The auditor studies how processes that produce and deliver the product are controlled, identified, measured, and monitored. The customer requirements and characteristics are important during this step of the audit trail. Nonconforming products are segregated and evaluated for disposition. Finally, the performance of the process is analyzed, and projects are chosen for improvement.

Links and samples. The common elements between each of the phases of this process are the products being sampled. The products could be the same ones that were sampled for new product development. The sampling should be conducted with the following considerations:

- Do the sampled products involve all the major processes?

- Do the sampled products represent the major product families?

Select some products that represent a small percentage of sales revenue and some that represent major product lines. This will determine whether the organization has applied its operational controls across the board. If the organization is required to provide any post-delivery services, that process will need to be sampled as well.

The measurement and monitoring devices (or *resources* as ISO 9001:2015 refers to them) used in the operations must be controlled according to clause 7.1.5, Monitoring and Measuring Resources. These devices measure the characteristics in the monitoring and measurement activities (clause 8.5.1a and c). The auditor should document several monitoring and measuring devices when auditing the production and service provision (clause 8.5), and then follow up with control of monitoring and measuring devices (clause 7.1.5) for calibration activities.

Finally, after product characteristics are measured, conforming products go to the next stage, and nonconforming products are segregated. These must follow a process described in clause 8.7, Control of Nonconforming Outputs.

F. *Support process.* The intent of this audit trail, which includes the shop floor audit, is to verify that an organization has effective control over its production and service operations. To do so, the organization has to set up a number of activities and mechanisms on the production floor. To audit these items, the auditor should proceed as follows:

- Ask for layout diagram of the plant.

- Ask for a production schedule.

- Sample departments (that is, part numbers) to audit. In a representative sample of key products and processes, include receiving, final inspection, and packaging.

- Ask for a process flowchart and inspection plan, if applicable; if not, then try to construct one or understand their inspection plan in each process step.

- Sample processes to audit.

The following assessments should be made for each process sampled in the process flow:

- Study the operator work instructions or documented information (clause 8.5.1a).
- Ask the operator how he or she operates and sets up the machine.
- Study responses versus work instructions.
- Ask how the organization inspects its product.
- Check the inspection plan or equivalent against what is being performed.
- Ask about gages mastered and write down gage numbers.
- Check the gage calibration sticker or its equivalent for a calibration date. Has it expired?
- Check the tagging procedure (product identification and traceability, clause 8.5.2) and/or work instructions. Check visually throughout the department.
- What does the operator do about nonconforming parts? Check this response against their documented nonconforming procedure (clause 8.7).
- Check inspection status as appropriate.
- Write down operator names, operation numbers, gage numbers, and document numbers for the audit trail.
- At the end of the interview, ask to see production records. Sample weeks of data for each operation for conformity. Note: This is key to the provision audit trail.
- Ask about the quality policy.
- Ask about process changes.
- Look at the overall cleanliness of the plant and the maintenance process. (Note: packaging and shipping areas should be examined as well.)

G. *Performance-based audits.* These start with performance-based audit plans in the stage 1 audit. Performance-based audits focus on the process in question and use a turtle diagram that probes competence, resources, inputs, outputs, and measurement/monitoring of the process, competence, and resources. They ask the question of whether the process measures are aligned with the overall objectives/mission/vision of the organization, and also whether the company is succeeding in meeting their targets and whether they are improving.

The turtle diagram and a process analysis tool will be used in the performance-based audit. This book will provide an excerpt of a conformance checklist. The entire checklist could not be included due to ISO 9001:2015 copyright issues. See Appendix D. Performance-based audits are now a requirement of ISO 9001:2015, which is looking for QMS performance starting with the planning audit trail and then for each process performed.

Overall QMS Performance

The overall performance of the QMS needs to be planned in clause 6.1 (see planning audit trail) and quality objectives need to be defined and implemented. Top management is asked to take on accountability for QMS effectiveness, engage, direct, and support subordinates to meet QMS effectiveness, and ensure that the QMS achieves its intended results. There is no question on where the standard stands in terms of expectations for top management with respect to QMS effectiveness. The standard requires the organization to conduct a review and evaluate the performance and effectiveness of the QMS. Furthermore, there needs to be evidence of the results, and it needs to be reviewed in the management review. The planning audit trail will ensure the QMS performance and determine whether the organization is meeting its quality objectives and/or achieving its "intended results" (see Figure 2.6).

Process Performance

Clause 4.4. lays out detailed requirements on how processes need to be structured, address risk, be measured and monitored, and include performance indicators. It also requires the organization to evaluate a process and make changes if it is not achieving intended results. Process performance now is also a requirement of the organizational roles and responsibilities in clause 5.3 of the standard. Process performance, though separated from the other audit trails, needs to be considered when each process is audited. Process performance audits, along with QMS performance audits, can also be conducted by themselves.

CONDUCTING A PROCESS PERFORMANCE AUDIT

The process performance audit starts with the auditor checking the structure of the process, that is, process owner and process linkages. Next, the auditor walks through the turtle diagram (see Figure 2.11) and documents the inputs and outputs of the process, the performance indicators, documented information, and the infrastructure of the process. The performance indicator and the overall objective and/or QMS performance indictor are documented and reviewed. What overall objective is this process trying to help achieve? Are there risk and opportunities identified for the process? Are the actions implemented? Did it mitigate the risk and help accomplish the overall objective?

Is the process performing satisfactorily? If the process performance has not been met, are there changes planned? Did these actions improve the process?

The turtle diagram is integrated into the Process Analysis Worksheet.

Completing the Process Analysis Worksheet

A Process Analysis Worksheet as shown in Figure 2.12 should be used to record the objective evidence identified during the process performance audit. It's a good idea to complete as much of the

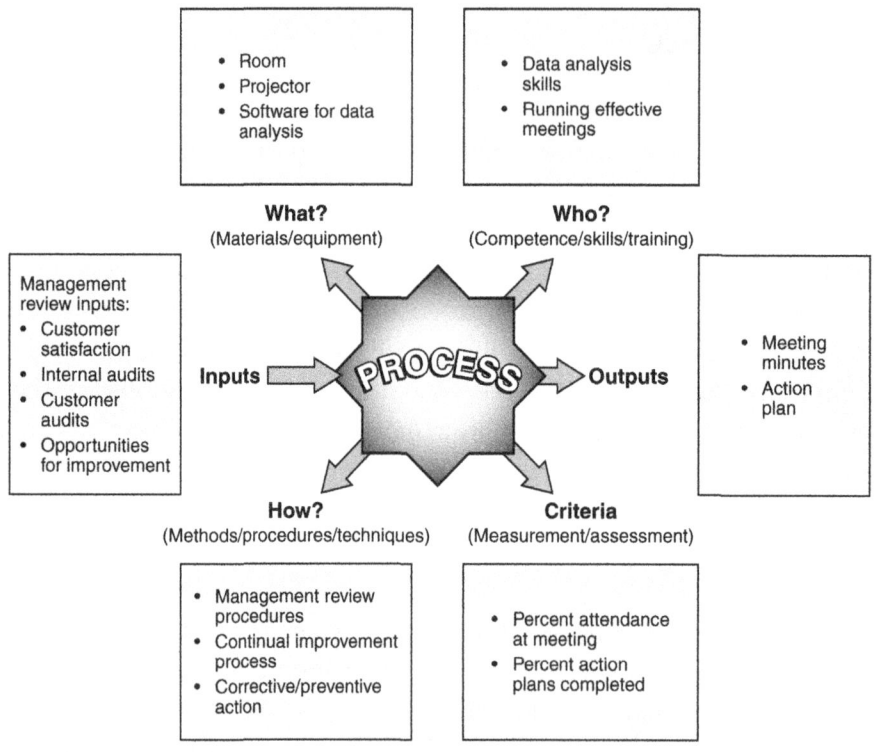

Figure 2.11 Turtle diagram.

Process Analysis Worksheet as possible prior to the audit for the processes selected. This includes figuring out which questions should be asked. When a suspect or poorly performing process has been identified, it should become the auditor's primary focus.

Prepare the process-related questions during stage 1:

- Identify all the process concerns as they relate to performance issues for the customer and/or overall organizational performance. Study the process to see if there is an explanation for the QMS performance issue, customer-related issue, scorecard, or satisfaction survey.

- Second, identify the general process-related and/or risk-related questions as they arise in stage 1.

- Third, identify potential questions relating to ISO 9001:2015 conformance.

When completing the Process Analysis Worksheet be sure to:

- Complete the header with company name and location. (A, B)

- Identify the type of audit—for example, system, process, product, or supplier—and the applicable standard. (C, D)

- Identify auditor name. (E)

Process Analysis Worksheet				
Company name: (A)	Location: (B)	Audit type: (C)		Standard: (D)
Auditor name: (E)			Process: (F)	
Responsibilities/Process owner (clause 4.4.1e) (G)			Process linkages (Predecessor) Subsequent process (clause 4.4.1b) (H)	
Applicable clauses: (I) Related quality objective or QMS performance metric: (K)			(J) *Process diagram: What? (Materials/equipment), Who? (Competence/skills/training), Inputs → PROCESS → Outputs, How? (Methods/procedures/techniques), Criteria (Measurement/assessment)*	
Related risk and opportunities analysis: ❏ Yes ❏ Not applicable (L)				
Are the actions implemented? ❏ Yes ❏ No Explain: (L)				
Is the organization meeting process performance indicators? ❏ Yes ❏ No (M)				
If no, are there planned changes? ❏ Yes ❏ No (M)				
Are the changes effective? That is, is the process showing improvement? Explain: (M)				
Objective evidence: (N) (What was sampled?)			Objective evidence: (N) Customer-specific requirements applicable: (O)	

Figure 2.12 Process analysis worksheet.

- Identify the process and area being audited. Since it is a prioritized audit, processes chosen typically affect customer satisfaction, customer complaints, or organizational performance issues. (F)

- Who has overall responsibility for the process? We would like to see one process owner although it is not a requirement of ISO 9001:2015. However, effectiveness and ownership are important. Are they able to answer the questions in regard to the process? (G)

- Identify the interfaces or links of the process with other processes. Does the process documentation show the links, and does the client understand them? You should also summarize the process details. (H)

- Determine which clauses of ISO 9001:2015 the process satisfies. A process could easily satisfy multiple clauses. (I)

- The turtle diagram (J) can be used during the interview to audit the process. See Figure 2.11 for how to fill out a turtle diagram.

- Identify the quality objectives or overall QMS performance that this process is related to. Is the process performance indicator customer focused, that is, when the process indicator improves, will it improve the QMS performance indicator to achieve the objective? (K)

- Was risk analysis performed as it relates to the process being investigated? Are the actions related to risk for the process implemented? Document the risk-related action and what was done. (L)

- Is the process performing satisfactorily? If it is not, are changes identified and implemented? (M)

- Are the changes effective, that is, is the process improving? (M)

- The objective evidence should capture samples taken to ensure that the process conforms to the requirements (clauses, see [I]). This area in the worksheet is also used to capture notes from the stage 1 audit as it relates to the process in question. (N)

- Determine which customer and customer-specific quality management system requirements affect the process. Also identify all statutory and regulatory requirements. (O)

3
Conducting the Stage 1 Audit for ISO 9001:2015

All audits, whether internal, second party, or third party, need to conduct a stage 1 audit. Stage 1 audits are performed on-site, working with the auditee whenever possible. The stage 1 audit consists of the following, at a minimum:

a. *Documented information review (document review).* The documented information review is typically conducted the first time a system is assessed. The documented information review assesses the "process approach" of the organization and studies the "documented information" of the organization. ISO 9001:2015 has no requirements for a quality manual, or procedures. There are requirements for processes to cover the "shalls" of the standard. Processes may or may not be documented, but still need to be planned and carried out in a controlled manner. More on documentation review later.

b. *Performance analysis.* The performance data of the organization, including customer scorecards, customer satisfaction data, and management review key performance indicators (KPIs), need to be studied to understand what processes are not performing. These "suspect processes" will need to be studied in turn to determine whether they are performing or not.

c. *Audit plan.* The audit plan needs to be completed as one of the last steps of the stage 1 audit. A process-based audit plan can be completed if an organization has a good process map or process approach.

d. *Feasibility review.* The feasibility of the audit can be understood best by studying the process approach, management review, and internal audits. If the organization is not ready, then it behooves the stage 2 audit to be postponed.

e. *Process analysis worksheet.* Auditors can use an audit plan for the stage 1 audit (Figure 3.1). This book recommends its use as a good practice. It is not unusual to have a one- or two-day stage 1 audit depending on the organization's size.

Date	Time	Activity	Who	Comment for reader
	30 minutes	Opening meeting		
	1 hour	Facility tour (optional)		Not required for internal audits
	3 or more hours	Process approach and documented information review		Is the company process focused? Is there adequate documented information for the size and complexity of the business? Only performed typically in the first audit of a third-party audit. Subsequent audits will study documented information, but it will vary based on the audit.
	2 hours	Performance analysis—customer performance information (scorecards), business KPIs, customer complaints, process performance		Data are used to prioritize the audit and to understand performance issues related to the organization and its processes.
	2 or more hours	Management review, planning, and risks and opportunities, internal audits, and corrective action		Decision on whether to continue to stage 2 (feasibility of the audit) or postpone audit. Does the management system appear to be implemented and mature? Is the system mature enough to have "retained documented information" or records. In many instances, even though the auditee does not appear ready—for example, in an internal or second-party audit—the audit may need to proceed for continual improvement purposes. Due to cost considerations for travel, stage 1 and stage 2 audits may be held back to back. If stage 1 and stage 2 are held back to back, then some redundant stage 1 items may be skipped.
	3 or more hours	Audit planning and audit notes		Prioritize the audit based on the performance data, and also make notes on process weaknesses identified and areas that need to be investigated.
	30 minutes	Closing meeting		Closing meeting

Figure 3.1 Stage 1 audit plan.

DOCUMENTED INFORMATION REVIEW

The organization's documented information needs to be studied to understand how it meets the requirements of the standard—for their process approach and to "maintain documented information to support the operation of its processes" (clause 4.4.2).

Since there are no longer any requirements for documentation, the auditor needs to accept the documentation and structure provided by the organization during the stage 1 assessment. It is safe to assume that companies will not abandon the structure of a quality manual, process documentation, and work instructions that has been adopted and that has been prevalent in industry for many years (see Figure 3.2).

As a first step in reviewing the documented information, it is best to study the process approach of the organization. Once the processes and their "sequence and interaction" are identified, the auditor can determine to what extent they are documented and whether they support the "operation of its processes" (clause 4.4.2) and whether the auditor agrees that the amount of documentation is adequate for the "effectiveness of the quality management system" (clause 7.5.1). The amount of

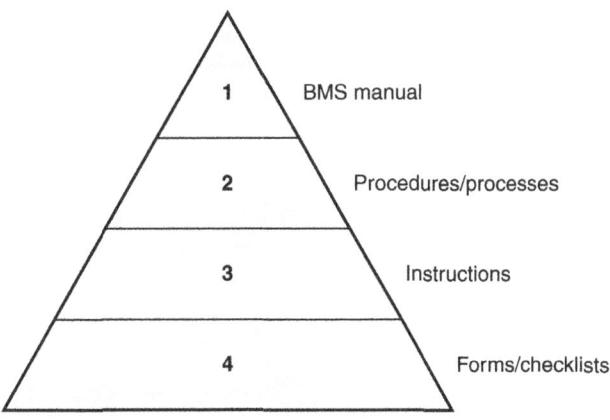

Figure 3.2 Typical structure of ISO documentation.

documentation necessary for effectiveness is really a stage 2, on-site audit determination; however, the auditor can start formulating the decision in stage 1 of the audit itself.

PROCESS APPROACH

The process approach is implicit in the ISO 9001:2015 standard. The process approach is described by ISO 9001:2015 in clause 0.3.1 in the non-normative section as follows: "The process approach involves the systematic definition and management of processes, and their interactions, so as to achieve the intended results in accordance with the quality policy and strategic direction of the organization." his is the picture Omnex uses to explain how the interaction of the QMS processes supports the organization in meeting its goals and objectives and overall strategic direction as defined by the mission, vision, and policies.

In auditing the process approach, the auditor is going to evaluate the (1) sequence and interaction of the processes, and (2) process linkages or interfaces.

SEQUENCE AND INTERACTION OF THE PROCESSES

The auditor should study the organization's process map or equivalent during the audit (Figure 3.3). Is the process map location-specific and does it explain the processes in the organization being audited? Many processes connect between on-site and remote locations. Business planning, objectives deployment, management reviews, new product development, purchasing, and sales are a few processes that have the potential of crossing functional and geographical areas. Sample the process documents. Are the interfaces of the processes clearly identified between locations, or do the documents stop within the four walls of the site or support function?

- Process maps should be simple but descriptive enough to show the sequence and interaction of processes.

38 Chapter Three

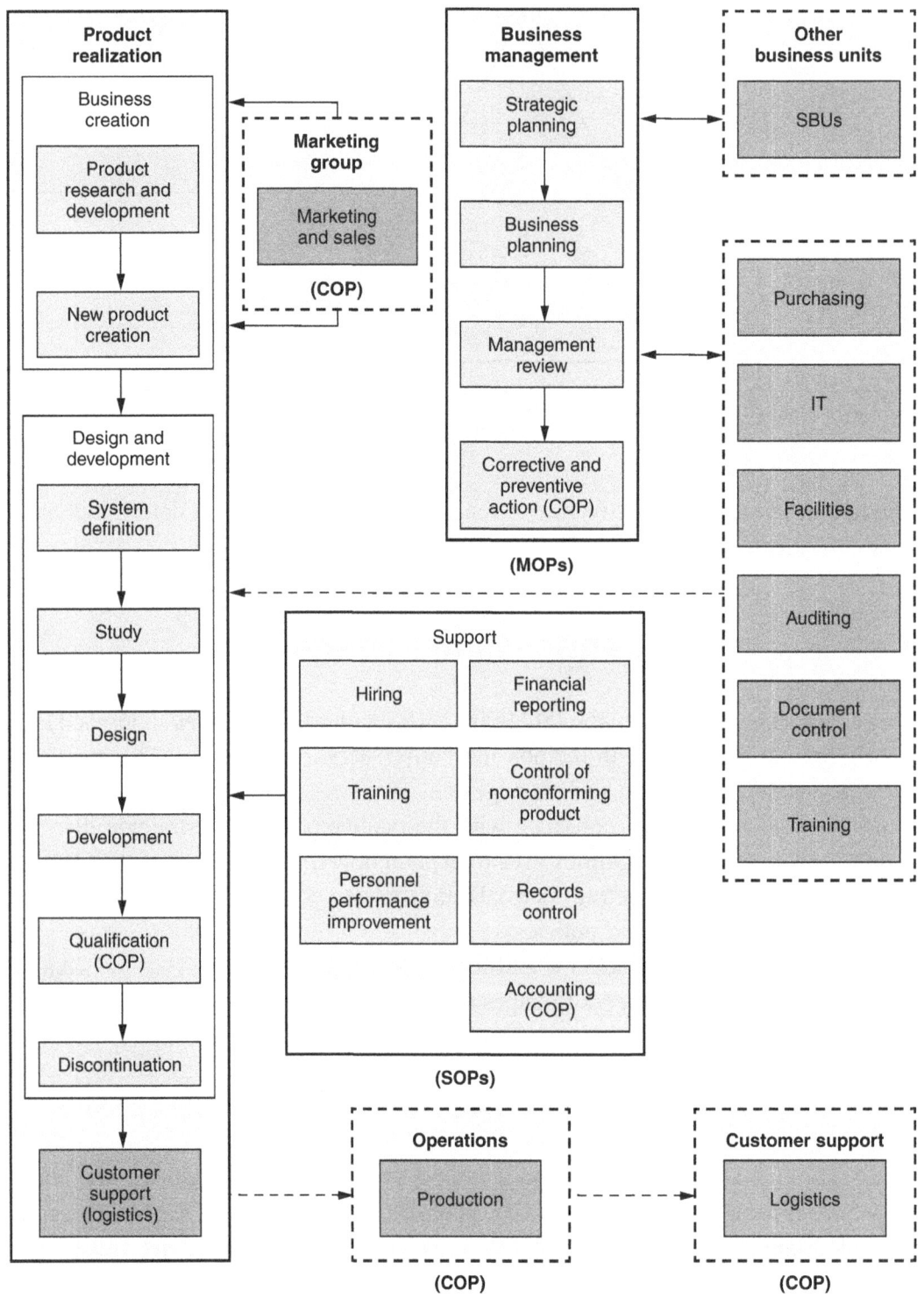

Figure 3.3 Process map example.

- The process map processes are meta-processes that flow into several lower-level processes typically documented in the level II procedures.

- Is there a process map that shows how all of the entities link together and how the overall processes link corporate headquarters, sales, design, manufacturing, assembly, and the warehouse?

- Does the 'organization's process map show the sequence and interaction of the processes at the work site or entity?

PROCESS LINKAGES OR PROCESS INTERFACES

The auditor must examine the links for multiple processes between the site and remote locations, as well as within the entity being audited. Do the inputs and outputs match? Does the process interface make sense relative to the process being studied? In the previous chapter, seven audit trails were introduced that will help auditors evaluate links and samples that can check these interfaces within each audit trail.

Note: The auditor should be aware of a process approach versus an elemental, departmental, or functional approach. Processes identified by the organization should not be repeats of the clauses in ISO 9001 and should not be departmental or functional processes (see Figures 3.4 and 3.5).

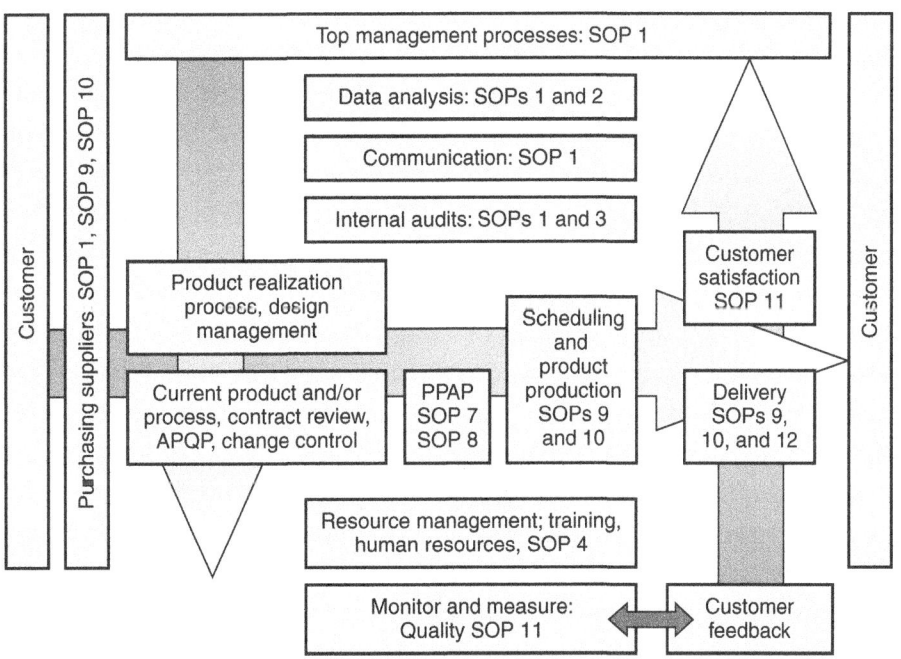

Figure 3.4   Clause or elemental process map.

Study the process map overall. Ensure that it is not clause and/or function focused and that it fully explains the organization, including on-site and/or remote locations. Support processes could include business planning, new product development, purchasing, sales, and warehousing.

If there is a process common to the support location and the work site, answer the following questions:

- Is process continuity maintained between the support location and the work site?
- Are there two process owners or one?
- How is the process managed, measured, or improved?
- Is the shared process equally applicable to both the support location and the work site?
- Do the outputs of the support process input directly to the on-site process, and vice versa?
- If there are two processes, one for the support location and one for the work site, are the inputs and outputs of each process clearly defined?

Note: The auditor must obtain a copy of the process description that shows all the interactions and attach it to the audit report.

CLAUSE- OR FUNCTION-BASED PROCESS MAPS

Be careful about process map paradigms, process versus clauses, and process versus functions. The auditor should be aware of a process approach versus a clause, departmental, or functional approach to developing processes (see Figure 3.4). Processes identified by the organization shouldn't be repeats of the clauses in ISO 9001:2015. They also shouldn't be departmental or functional processes. Figure 3.4 shows an elemental approach, and Figure 3.5 shows a functional approach.

The process map shown in Figure 3.4 is predominantly clause oriented. Its monitoring and measuring, resource management, FAI, product realization, communication, internal audits, and data analysis elements are simply clauses of the ISO 9001:2008 standard. Furthermore, the process map shows no interactions and thus fails to document how the organization actually operates.

However, this map does illustrate the "quality paradigm" of professionals who have worked with standards since the days of the MIL standards. Many organizations have used procedures developed by quality professionals based on standards requirements from the 1980s. The quality paradigm makes it impossible for implementers or auditors to see beyond the requirements (of standards) to the processes that allow the organization to function.

Process performance must also be examined. Evaluate the process performance data. According to ISO 9001:2000, clause 3.2.14, effectiveness is the extent to which planned activities are realized and planned results achieved; according to clause 3.2.15, efficiency is the relationship between the results achieved and resources used.

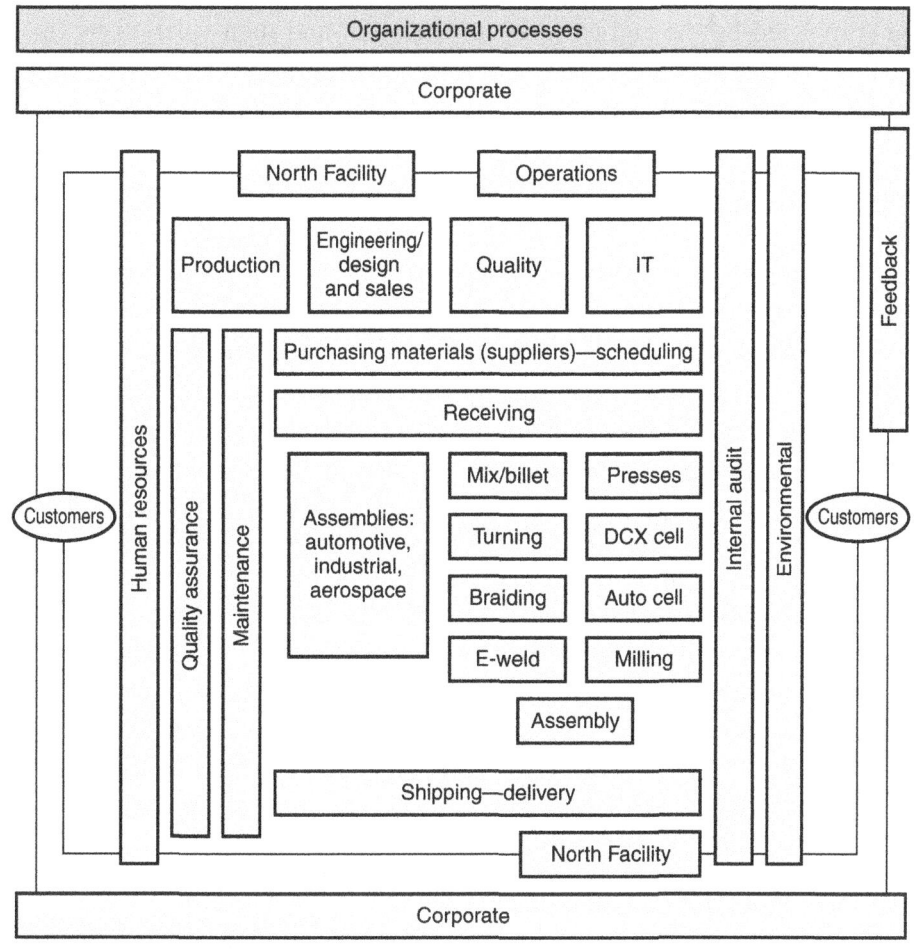

Figure 3.5 Functional process map.

There's a big difference between product/process performance and business performance (key indicators and performance trends). The latter is focused more on business results than the former is.

Figure 3.5 shows a process map that's based on the departments and functions of the plant. Instead of documenting processes, it shows the many departments in the plant, such as engineering, quality, information technology (IT), human resources, and production. Processes aren't functions or departments, although they do cut across them. This map also fails to indicate interactions between its various elements.

A. DOCUMENTED INFORMATION REVIEW

Study the product realization process and the support processes. Does the process list take into consideration all the clauses and sub-clauses of ISO 9001:2015? The audit checklist in Appendix B (Figure B.4) provides a list (matrix) of sub-clauses and their associated processes. This list or

42 Chapter Three

matrix can be completed by the auditee prior to the audit and then verified by the auditor. Note: This is a high-level check, and the auditor will look in detail at processes during the documented information review.

Process Documentation

ISO 9001:2015 does not require that any processes are documented, but requires the organization to have adequate documentation for the operation of its processes and for effectiveness (clauses 4.4.2 and 7.5.1). The auditor can study the documentation presented in the conformance checklist to ensure it covers all the requirements of the specific clauses or sub-clauses that the organization claims the documented processes cover. Note: Due to copyright issues with ISO, the full checklist could not be included in this book. One page is provided in Appendix D.

- Study each "shall" of the ISO 9001 clause (the checklist identifies) and the organization's customer-specific requirement document. Are these requirements addressed in the process documentation? In other words, does it give a sense of what they do to implement a requirement (that is, "shall")? Note 1: Auditors should not accept process documentation that simply quotes the standard verbatim. Note 2: If process documentation covers a process, the auditor expectation is that it should cover all the "shalls" unless a viable explanation is provided to the contrary. Note 3: A customer-specific requirement is a specific requirement for the quality management system processes, product requirements, and testing requirements made by the customer.

- If the documentation does not explain how the organization addresses a "shall," ask the auditee to show how he or she addresses it.

- The process documentation must describe *what* the organization does, *who* does it, and *when* it's done. The "what" must describe the process steps.

- A process, as described in the introduction of ISO 9001:2015, has inputs, activities (or process steps), outputs, and checkpoints. The introduction (non-normatives) suggests that "monitoring and measuring checkpoints, which are necessary for control, are specific to each process and will vary depending on the related risks." See Figure 3.6 (from the Introduction to ISO 9001:2015).

Note: A process is *not* a clause or element of ISO 9001. A process will probably not be confined within a single organizational department. In fact, it may not even be confined within the building!

When reviewing a process document, look for the following (ISO 9001:2015 clause 4.4.1 explicitly asks for the following):

- Inputs and outputs.

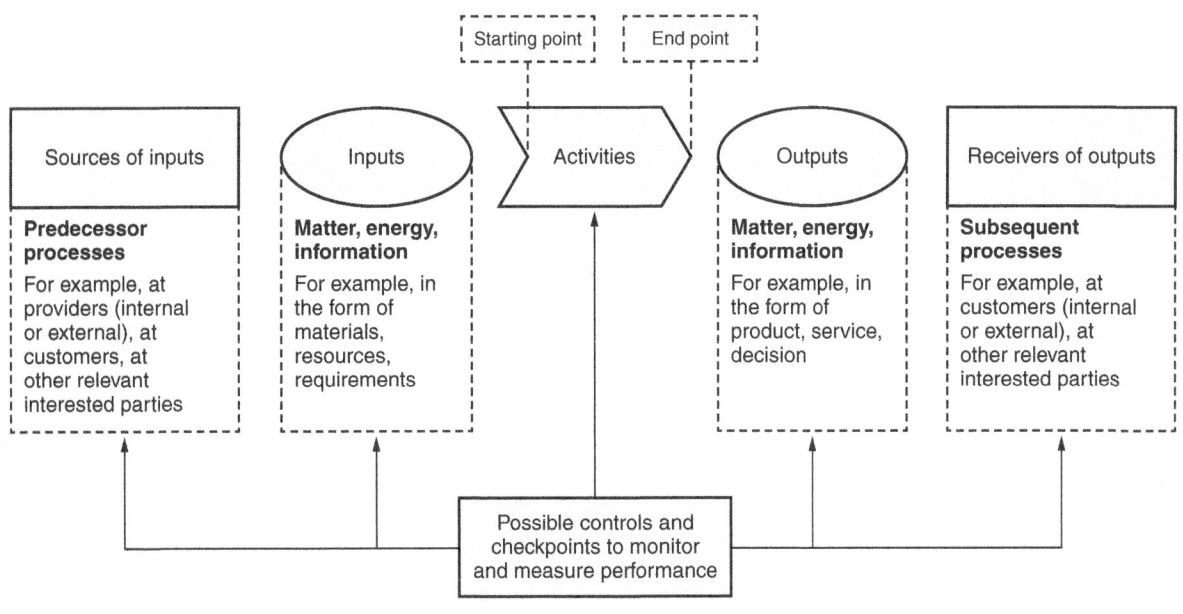

Figure 3.6 Schematic representation of the elements of a single process.

- Criteria and methods (monitoring, measuring, and performance indicators). Some measures could be for control and others could be for process performance.

- Responsibilities and authorities (who does what—should be a title).

- Risks and opportunities as they relate to planning (clause 6.1). Note, this will not be in the process documentation, but the organization should be able to provide the risk assessment.

- Includes retained documented information as necessary, that is, records.

- Ensure that processes are delivering their "intended outputs" or performing (clause 5.3b). Check whether there are records showing they are being monitored.

The remainder of clause 4.4.1 is evaluated during stage 2 of the audit, that is:

- Evaluate and make changes to meet process goals and objectives ("intended results")

- Improve the processes and the QMS

Keep in mind that clause 4.4.1 requirements are for all processes whether they are documented or not. Processes that are not documented will be evaluated for clause 4.4.1 requirements via the Process Analysis Worksheet.

- Update the documentation and process cross-reference (Figure B.4).

B. PERFORMANCE ANALYSIS

Study customer satisfaction (perception), customer satisfaction supplemental (scorecards), customer complaints and problem solving, and overall performance (or KPIs) of the organization. Poorly performing indicators or metrics represent lack of "intended results" or customer dissatisfaction with the organization, both requirements of clauses 6.1.1 (planning) and 5.1.2, Customer Focus.

An ISO 9001 audit begins with the auditor analyzing overall customer satisfaction and organizational performance. Lack of results or poorly performing indicators are then linked by the auditor to poorly performing or suspect processes. These also could be an indicator of poor risk analysis and/or implementation of actions in regard to risk and opportunities. These are documented in the Process Analysis Worksheet. The auditor also takes these results into consideration when auditing management review and/or process performance and investigates how the organization responds when performance falls short.

Customer Scorecards

Poor customer scorecards and poor performance relative to customer expectations are indicators of potentially severe customer dissatisfaction. The auditor is required to study the performance relative to all subscribing customers. If they have an online scorecard, the auditor is required to study the most current data and ascertain the supplier score.

Be careful when reviewing these data, since each customer has a different rating system. Many times the customer is happy with one commodity or one set of parts and not another commodity or another set of parts. It is easy to show the auditor just the good data and bamboozle him/her if he/she does not really understand the products and/or the customer's method for reckoning scorecards. It is important that the auditor know all the products supplied to a particular customer and ensure that the data relative to all the products gets reviewed online, live on the customer website.

The auditor should make a record of the quality issues, warranty issues, and delivery problems identified in the scorecards, product by product. Each of these issues must be tracked and audited (see Figure 3.7).

Having no problems in customer metrics or customer scorecards does not necessarily mean high satisfaction. Bottom line—satisfaction can only be gauged by getting the customer perception. This entails asking the customer to answer some variant of the question, "Overall, how satisfied are you with us?"

The auditor shall review the following, at a minimum, for each customer:

- Identify all organizational key customers.

- From the list of customers, identify which customers provide scorecards. For each customer, review the customer scorecard online. Carefully identify which customers score by plant and which customers score by product line. Don't be satisfied by reviewing printed-out materials because they could be misleading.

Information from Customer Scorecard					
Customer	Customer quality performance	Customer/ assembly plant disruptions	Delivery schedule performance	Other	Risk analysis conducted (Y/N)

Figure 3.7 Information from customer scorecard.

Assessment Planning Table	
Customer and performance issues	Related suspect processes

Figure 3.8 Assessment planning table.

- Identify all customer performance issues. Particularly, determine whether the customer has put them into a special status category for improvement.
- For each customer, ask the organization how it evaluates "overall satisfaction." (Note: Scorecard performance isn't the same as customer satisfaction.)

For any customer scorecard category where the organization's performance doesn't meet the customer expectation and/or goal, document the category and related suspect processes in the Assessment Planning Table (Figure 3.8).

Customer Complaints and Problem-Solving Efforts

The auditor should look for patterns of the same problem repeating among common parts and/or many seemingly random returns, which may indicate a lack of process control for a single product.

The auditor should study how the organization prioritizes issues. Does it analyze Pareto charts? Are they analyzing data by part groups or process groups? If the organization does not analyze the data meaningfully for problem solving, that may be grounds for a nonconformity or an opportunity for improvement. Having many problems, or ones that continue unchecked, is also an indicator of poor problem-solving capabilities or process control issues. Find out how the organization calculates parts per million (ppm) levels. The auditor should analyze the customer complaint database to sample issues for an audit trail. Continual problems on one issue or part number, or many different problems for one part or part family or department, indicate potential samples for the auditor.

The key to solving customer-related problems and issues is the analysis of customer-related data, with prompt reaction to customer issues. When assessing the readiness of the organization, the auditor should not only evaluate customer-related issues, but also how the organization responds to them.

Intended Results and Customer Satisfaction

Overall, customer satisfaction issues, customer scorecard issues, and customer complaints on product quality all indicate potential customer dissatisfaction. These issues should all be investigated during the on-site audit. Organized KPIs may also prove to be indicators of potential issues in performance.

The auditor can translate these issues into on-site process investigations in the stage 2 audit, as shown later in the stage 1 audit (see Figure 3.8).

Note 1: Have the same customer satisfaction issues been identified by the organization and risk analysis performed as required by clause 5.1.2?

Note 2: These same problems must be repeated in Figure 3.8.

Evaluate Internal Audits and System Audit Results

Internal Audits. Internal audits are a good gauge of how well the organization understands itself. The auditor is reviewing the internal audit to ensure that the organization has conducted a complete system audit that includes all the processes and all the clauses of ISO 9001. The organization is expected to have 12 months of audit history, especially after the initial audit registration.

Audits should be scheduled based on status, importance, and the organization's annual plan. Also, the audits must be based on customer complaints, internal/external performance data, and how the internal audit has considered the customer-specific quality management system requirements.

Study the quality of the audit and the nonconformities issued. Does the internal audit include all the issues noticed in the organization thus far? Is the audit adequate? The nonconformities issued should have three parts: nonconformity, quote of the relevant requirement, and the objective evidence. What is the quality of the nonconformities; are they clear and concise?

Check out the quality of the nonconformity closeouts. Is there objective evidence to show that the corrective action has been implemented? Also, is there evidence that the system corrective actions have been implemented? Is there evidence to show that the problem will not repeat?

System Audit. System audits are conducted periodically (minimum once a year) to provide top management a snapshot review of the quality management system. System audits should be conducted with the same formality as third-party audits and should use the same processes and time durations as an initial audit. System audits should cover all the process map processes and all the clauses in ISO 9001:2015. Note: System audits are not a series of short audits conducted monthly, but are a snapshot in time of the overall health and vitality of the QMS.

The intent of these audits is to ascertain whether the overall system is "effective and efficient." This is the formal audit, which needs to be conducted similarly to an external audit. In this audit, the auditors are ensuring that the organization is moving toward its goals and objectives and customers are being satisfied.

Process Approach versus Clause or Elemental Approach

The audit must follow the process approach of the organization (see Figure 3.3). The audit plan must have processes from the organization's process map. Processes aren't chosen randomly, but are prioritized based on risks to the customer (for example, customer satisfaction, customer complaints).

QMS Performance

The QMS performance is evaluated in the *risk and opportunity* and *planning, performance evaluation, and improvement* (PEI) audit trails. Both of these audit trails introduced in Chapter 2 can be initiated during the stage 1 audit. To evaluate the QMS performance, start with the risk and opportunity audit trail. There is no need to ask for the process owner; the persons responsible for the stage 1 audit can answer the questions. Identify key interested party expectations and issues; are there related objectives? Discuss with the auditee how the objectives were chosen. What are the related risks and opportunities to ensure success in meeting them? What is the plan for meeting the objectives? What are the related processes for the risk in planning? See Figure 3.9.

In Figure 3.10, the same quality objectives as above are reviewed for their plans, how they are deployed within the organization, and whether the management review shows evidence that the objectives are being met. Figure 3.10 is a part of the PEI audit trail explained in Chapter 2.

The organization's overall performance must be gauged by examining records of management review. Note: Sometimes, auditees only conduct a management review once a year to comply with ISO 9001 and then only do it to show the records to the auditor. This type of "compliance" for such an important requirement should be duly recognized as a major nonconformity.

Risk Sampling Sheet					
Related interested party expectations* and internal/external issues (4.1 and 4.2)	Objectives and/or intended results (6.1.1)	Related risk and opportunities (6.1.1)	Plan to address risk and opportunities (6.1.2)	Related processes (6.1.2)	Evidence of actions implemented and effectiveness tracked (9.3.2)

*Note: Which internal and external issues and expectations are key to the organization? Has the organization adequately handled these expectations and issues when they set the objectives or "intended results"?

Figure 3.9 Risk sampling sheet.

Quality Objectives Sampling Sheet			
Quality objectives	Plan for meeting objectives (what will be done, resources, who is responsible, when it will be completed, how results will be evaluated) (6.2.1)	Deployed objectives (sample department and identify deployed objectives)	Objective evidence of objectives being met and actions completed (9.3.2)

*Quality objectives relate to the needs and expectations of interested parties and could result in objectives related to product quality, on-time delivery, or other expectations critical to an interested party, including customers. Note: Clause 6.2.1 requires quality objectives to be consistent with quality policy, be measurable, satisfy requirements, be relevant to products/services and customer satisfaction, and be monitored, communicated, and updated.

Figure 3.10 Quality objectives sampling sheet.

The management review must be conducted at suitable intervals to assess overall improvements and to note whether the organization is meeting business objectives and satisfying its customer needs and expectations. It is important for the auditor to note whether the management review is just a presentation of facts or is a meeting that is improvement-oriented and evaluates the need for changes to the overall management system, quality policy, and objectives.

At a minimum, the management review or business review must cover these topics:

- Status of actions from previous management reviews

- Changes to external and internal issues (business context) that affect the quality management system

- Information on the performance and effectiveness and trends in:

  - Customer satisfaction and feedback from relevant interested parties.

  - Quality objectives, and whether they have been met (see Figure 3.10).

  - Process performance and product and service conformity.

  - Nonconformities and corrective actions.

  - Monitoring and measurement results (see clause 9.1.1; the organization needs to be explicit in what they monitor and measure, and the monitoring and measurement needs to evaluate the performance and effectiveness of the QMS).

  - Results of audits.

  - Performance of external providers.

The auditor shouldn't expect the organization to cover each topic during every business review. However, the topics must be covered according to top management requirements to move the organization forward. Also, it is important to evaluate the management review's output to ensure that it includes decisions and actions for improvement of the quality management system, changes to the QMS, and resource needs.

Overall performance should be gauged according to the "intended results" of the QMS (see clause 6.1.1a) and the quality objectives, and examining the business reviews that move the company forward on a weekly and monthly basis. Review the key indicators of the business, and note those that are performing poorly. Assess the overall quality of the business reviews. Is the company progressing toward its objectives? Also, do the objectives reflect customer/interested party needs, expectations, and key concerns? Review the risk and opportunity analysis conducted. How robust is the analysis? Will the actions mitigate risk? Have they been integrated back into the processes in the QMS?

Measuring Key Indicators and Performance Trends

Although it's not a requirement, the ISO 9001 auditor expectation is that the organization will measure trends on a chart that shows variables on the y-axis and months on the x-axis. Omnex recommends the use of trend charts, Pareto charts, and summaries of actions taken to improve a performance indicator.

Identify Suspect Processes

Based on the analysis of customer and performance data, identify poorly performing processes that create risk for the customer. Using the assessment planning table in Figure 3.8, analyze the customer supplemental, customer scorecards, management review performance data, and customer complaints. What are the key performance issues?

Identify the suspect processes that affect performance. Use the process identified in the process map to identify the relationship between intended results and process performance (see Figure 3.11). Prioritize the processes as they relate to product or process performance. Based on the analysis of the performance data, document processes that show weakness and require increased focus during the assessment planning stage.

The key performance indicators measuring the "intended outcomes" are supported by processes that enable them when the KPIs are not performing. The underlying cause of this is that the processes are not performing well. The auditor in stage 1 is identifying these "suspect processes" for a full investigation in stage 2 of the audit.

An audit plan should be organized according to the processes in the organization's process map, not by clauses in the standard. The audit plan should be prioritized according to "suspect"

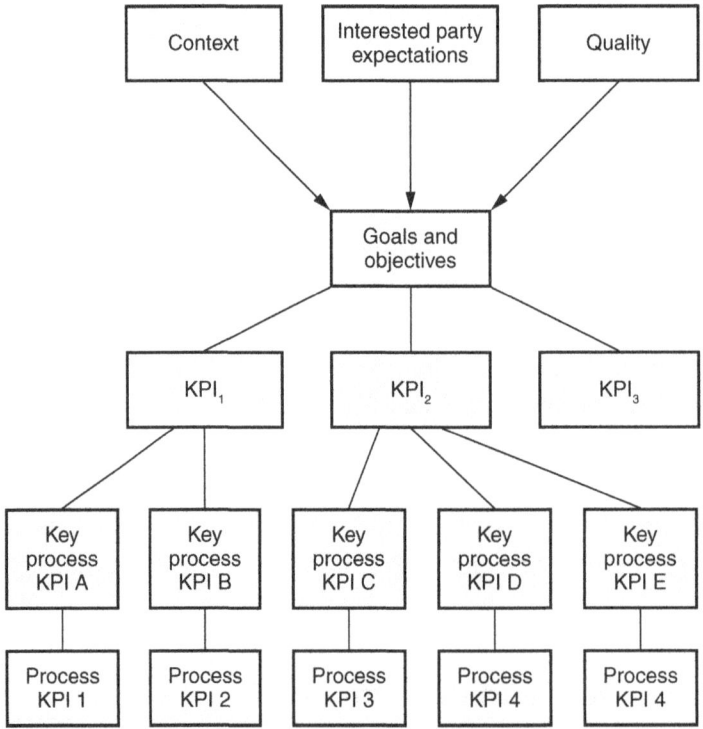

Figure 3.11 Planning, performance evaluation, and improvement audit trail.

processes identified during customer focus and performance analysis. Next, the auditor should identify the sequence of processes to audit by referring to the audit trails discussed in Chapter 2. Study the process map and identify the *planning, performance evaluation, and improvement* (PEI), *risk, new product development* (NPD), and *production and service provision* audit trails (provision).

C. CREATE AN AUDIT PLAN

Creating a prioritized audit plan based on weaknesses in customer and organizational performance is a key to a good audit (see Figure 3.12). Following the audit trails described in Chapter 2 is a good method for understanding linkages between processes and the ISO 9001 clauses, and for sample taking.

Audit the PEI processes, risk, and top management for leadership at the beginning of the audit:

- Start with context, interested party expectations, customer satisfaction, and scorecards; review top management's ideas about the key issues from the customer's viewpoint.

- Identify which auditor is the most proficient in each audit trail, and update the audit plans with the processes related to PEI, NPD, and provision audit trails.

- Identify all the organization's suspect processes to ensure they're included in the audit plans.

Stage 2 Audit Plan					
Objective: To verify conformance to ISO 9001:2015					
Date	Time	Auditor	Location	Organization's process # and/or description	Standard clauses
				Opening meeting	
				Facility tour	
				Review of context, interested party expectations, and planning, including risk	(4.1, 4.2, 6.1, 6.2)
				Review of customer needs and expectations, customer scorecard, associated corrective action, and customer satisfaction	(5.1.2, 9.1.2)
				Interview with top management	(5.1)
				Business/review	(9.3)

Figure 3.12 Stage 2 audit plan.

- Complete the documentation and process cross-reference for ISO 9001:2015 (see Figure B.4) and ensure that all clauses are being audited.

- Identify OEM and other customer-specific quality management system requirements and make notations in the audit plan to ensure that customer service representatives (CSRs) will be sampled.

- Audit based on the defined processes of the organization and not the ISO 9001 clauses.

- Begin with an audit of top management

When creating the audit plan, ensure that the following items are available for the audit:

- A description of the processes showing their sequence and interactions, including key indicators and performance trends for the previous 12 months, minimum

- Evidence that the organization's processes address all the requirements of ISO 9001:2015

- Internal audit and management review planning and results from the previous 12 months

- A list of customer-specific quality management system requirements

- Customer satisfaction and complaints status, including customer reports and scorecards

- Internal and external issues and interested party expectations

- Risk and opportunity analysis of intended results and products/processes that affect conformity and customer satisfaction

Finally, the auditor should keep in mind:

- Analysis of actual or potential risk to the customer, product, and processes

- Demonstration of links between audit trails

- Auditing manufacturing activities on the shifts

- Optimizing audit time based on the organization's layout

- Auditing support functions, with process links referenced planned on-site prior to the audit

- Customer-specific quality management system requirements and all relevant processes, including new customers since the last audit

- Customer concerns and/or complaints, special status notification, and the organization's response

- Internal audit and management review results and actions

- Progress made toward continual improvement

- Effectiveness of the corrective actions and verification implemented since the last audit

- QMS effectiveness with regard to achieving both customer and organizational objectives

- Distributing the audit plan to the organization and all audit team members

D. DETERMINE THE AUDIT FEASIBILITY

In third-party audits, the audit feasibility of the organization to proceed to stage 2 is determined in the stage 1 audit. If the organization isn't ready to conduct the stage 2 site audit, the certification body and the organization can agree to stop the process.

In the internal audit or a supplier audit, this is really not a choice. If the organization is not ready, the internal auditors can issue nonconformances that can be added to the final stage 2 audit report (see Figure 3.13). Stage 1 audit results shall be documented and communicated to the organization.

The stage 1 audit is the most critical step of the audit, so auditors should be thorough and provide nonconformities as necessary for improvement.

Nonconformities identified during this stage 1 audit.	
NC #	**Nonconformity description**

Figure 3.13 Stage 1—nonconformities.

For guidance to internal auditors, the following situations typically may require postponement in a third-party situation, or a major nonconformity in an internal audit situation:

- Customer scorecards show that the organization is under a special status category. Some of the customer-specific organizational approval statuses include limited approval, probation, suspension, or withdrawal.

- The organization doesn't have one year of internal audits, management reviews, or performance data.

- An internal system audit to ISO 9001:2015 (all processes, clauses, or aerospace process approach to audits) hasn't been completed.

- Management review shows no top management involvement, or the management review is incomplete.

- The organization shows poor customer or process focus.

- Documentation shows many requirements not being addressed by the organization's processes. Note: This is not implying that all processes be documented, but rather that documented processes need to cover all "shalls."

If there are obvious major nonconformities with respect to the implementation of the management system, and/or performance or customer issues, the auditor notes them and issues major nonconformities, or identifies them in the audit trails for the stage 2 audit.

E. PREPARE AND DELIVER THE STAGE 1 AUDIT REPORT

Internal and supplier auditors can identify any major or minor nonconformities and report them in the internal audit (Figure 3.13).

F. UPDATE PROCESS ANALYSIS WORKSHEET OR AUDIT CHECKLIST

The auditor should note all insights gained from the stage 1 audit on the Process Analysis Worksheet (Figure 3.14). All performance areas found to be deficient—whether QMS, objectives, process, or customer—should be noted on the Process Analysis Worksheet in the stage 2 audit. Areas of risk in question, and actions or plans not implemented, should be so noted.

Process Analysis Worksheet			
Company name:	Location:	Audit type:	Standard:
Auditor name:		Process:	
Reponsibilities/Process owner (clause 4.4.1e)		Process linkages (Predecessor) Subsequent process (clause 4.4.1b)	
Applicable clauses: Related quality objective or QMS performance metric:		*[Process diagram showing Inputs → PROCESS → Outputs, with What? (Materials/equipment), Who? (Competence/skills/training), How? (Methods/procedures/techniques), Criteria (Measurement/assessment)]*	
Related risk and opportunities analysis: ❏ Yes ❏ Not applicable			
Are the actions implemented? ❏ Yes ❏ No Explain:			
Is the organization meeting process performance indicators? ❏ Yes ❏ No			
If no, are there planned changes? ❏ Yes ❏ No			
Are the changes effective? That is, is the process showing improvement? Explain:			
Objective evidence: (What was sampled?)		Objective evidence: Customer-specific requirements applicable:	

Figure 3.14   Process analysis worksheet.

4

Stage 2: On-Site Audit

AUDIT PROCEDURE

All audits, including internal audits, are required to follow the guidelines provided in ISO 19011:2011. Because these requirements are covered in a standard internal or lead auditor course, they're not discussed here. This book covers requirements *not* found in ISO 19011:2011 for the stage 2 on-site audit.

The stage 2 flow diagram is shown in Figure 4.1. The steps for the stage 2 on-site audit are as follows:

A. Conduct audit of remote supporting functions (recommended)

B. Opening meeting

C. Conducting the audit:

    C.1 Conduct facility tour, if needed

    C.2 Study customer and organizational performance

    C.3 Meeting with top management

    C.4 Audit organizational processes

    C.5 Verify that all processes and clauses are audited

D. Write up nonconformities

E. Closing meeting:

    E.1 Determine audit team recommendations

    E.2 Prepare the draft report

    E.3 Conduct the closing meeting

58 Chapter Four

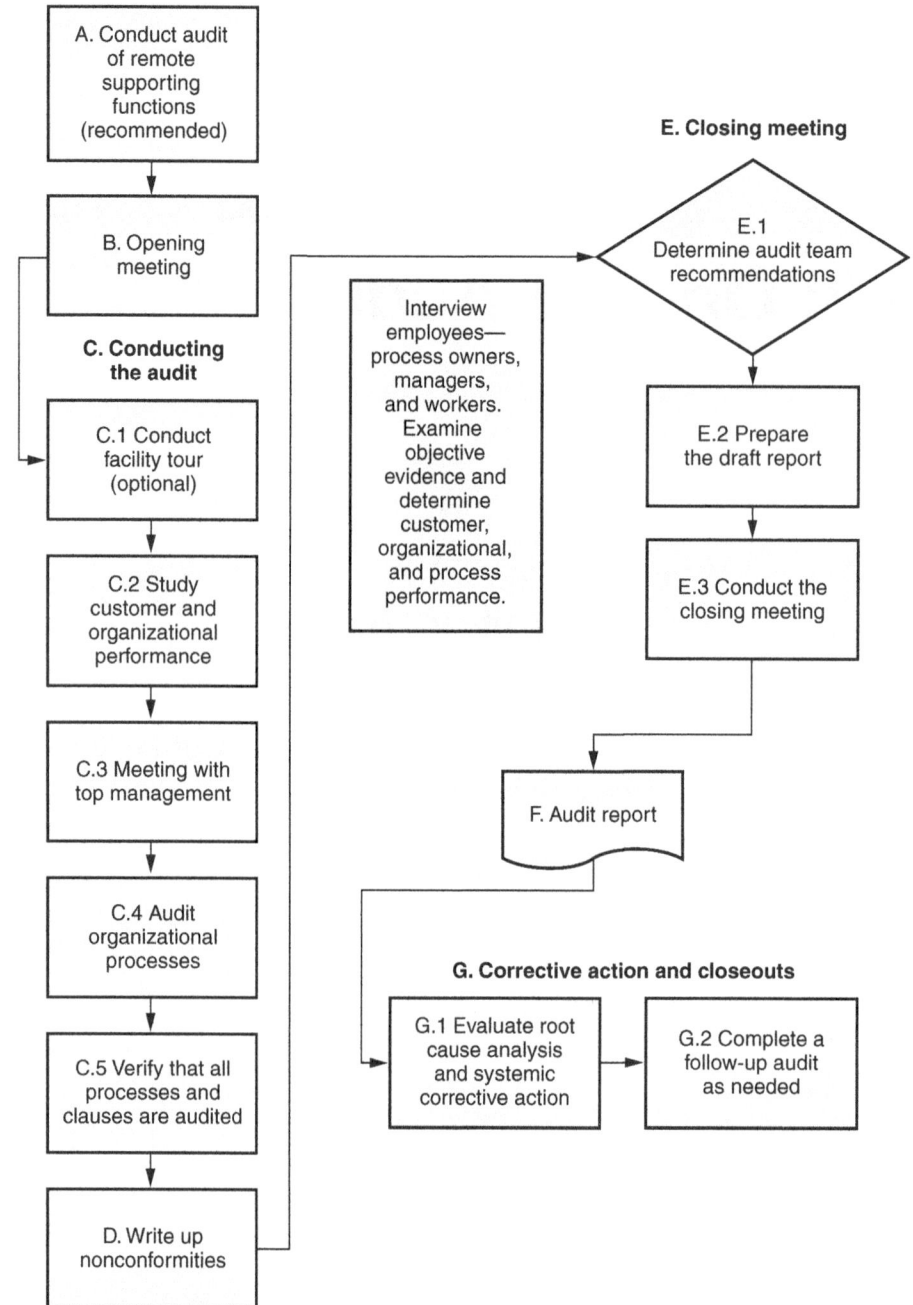

Figure 4.1 Stage 2 flow diagram.

F. Audit report

G. Corrective action and closeouts:

  G.1 Evaluate root cause analysis and systemic corrective action

  G.2 Complete a follow-up audit as needed

After the stage 1 audit, the auditor should continue following the prioritized audit plan, taking into consideration the performance issues noted during the on-site audit. Second, the auditor needs to determine whether the organization actually reflects the process-oriented nature of its process map and documentation information reviewed in stage 1, and whether the processes are performing. Finally, and most importantly, the auditor needs to assess whether the QMS is achieving its intended results and its overall quality objectives.

A. Conduct Audit of Remote Supporting Functions

Step A in Figure 4.1 is just a reminder that the supporting functions should be audited first as best practice before the on-site audit is conducted. All the steps of the stage 2 audit should be completed for these functions before the audit of the manufacturing site.

Many of the processes are initiated at the supporting functions and remote locations. The samples taken at the supporting functions can be followed to the site—whether they're sales, design, purchasing, or top management functions. Auditors need to keep in mind that they're starting at the supporting functions in order to check the interfaces between processes—whether it is in regard to deploying objectives or developing new product.

Auditor Requirements

- Identify the processes that provide a link between support functions and the site. These processes should be evident in the process map itself. Are they?

- Does the process documentation connect the site to the remote location?

- How is the process managed? Is it working effectively? Take samples for each of the processes that will be used to test the interface. Whether they involve top management objectives, new products in sales and/or design, or integrating customer satisfaction information into the sales office, carefully sample them and follow each process from the supporting function into the site. Does the process link to other processes? How is it measured, monitored, and improved? Are there dual persons responsible for the processes, that is, in the site and remote location? Are they working together? Are the performance indicators the same? Or is one person managing the process from start to finish?

- Audit the process using stage 2 step C.4—audit organizational processes. Are the supporting functions and sites working together? Are they designed to succeed together?

B. Opening Meeting

During step B, the opening meeting, the auditors are introduced to the organization's management team (see Figure 4.1). This gives auditors an opportunity to explain the overall auditing process, including process approach, risk management, and performance of the management system. ISO 19011:2002 contains detailed requirements for the opening meeting.

Auditor Requirements. During the opening meeting, the auditor needs to inform the auditee of the following items:

- Risk-based thinking and the process approach
- Audit plan
- Reconfirm the following:
  - Customer satisfaction and complaint status, including customer reports and scorecards
  - Supporting functions and interfacing processes
- Confirm the following:
  - The audit will encompass a cross-section of the organization from top management to middle management, workers, and engineers.
  - The audit will take place where the work is done and not in an office. Even if the records are computerized, the audit should be done in the cubicle of the engineer or the manager, as required.
  - Large crowds can't follow the auditor. These tend to skew the audit process. Why? Auditees need to be in a natural setting and made to feel at ease for the audit to be most successful.
  - The auditor will immediately point out nonconformities to the auditee.

See the Opening Meeting Checklist in Figure 4.2, which encompasses both the ISO 19011 and ISO 9001 requirements.

C. Conducting the Audit

When conducting the audit in step C, the auditor needs to follow all the points made during the opening meeting (see Figure 4.2). In other words, audit a cross-section of the organization, especially top management. Audit time should include and involve top management, especially for the *risk and opportunity* and PEI audit trails.

Involving the process owners in each of the interviews regarding the process during stage 2 is important. The process owner should be able to explain from the beginning to the end of the process, and how it is monitored, measured, improved, and resourced.

An illustration of this is an audit performed in a large Fortune 100 organization. Engineering changes were being audited in this organization. The manager introduced herself as the process owner and explained to the auditor that engineering changes were done using ERP software called

Opening Meeting Checklist
❏ Introduce audit team and attendees
❏ Pass out the attendance sheet
❏ Explain the risk and process approach
❏ Review objectives, scope, and criteria
❏ Review supporting functions and interfacing processes
❏ Summary of methods and procedures used for audit:
❏ Auditor takes notes of details for both conformities and nonconformities
❏ Audit conclusion is based on samples taken
• The audit will take a cross-section of the organization, from top management to maintenance workers and engineers
❏ The audit is restricted to small groups of three or fewer people
❏ The auditor notifies auditee of nonconformities during the audit as well as during a daily review meeting
❏ Questions should be directed toward lead auditor
❏ Conditions for when a major nonconformity affecting the customer is uncovered.
❏ Establish auditee communication link
❏ Reconfirm the following:
❏ Current customers and interested parties
❏ Customer satisfaction and complaint status, including customer reports and scorecards
❏ Any customer special status (bad supplier status)
❏ Supporting functions and interfacing processes
❏ Review prioritized audit plan
❏ Confirm status of stage 1 issues, including documentation
❏ Confirm time and date of closing meeting
❏ Confirm relevant safety, emergency, and security procedures.

Figure 4.2 Opening meeting checklist.

SAP. She was asked how many of the change requests originated with the customer. She replied with mild irritation that she just took care of the changes and didn't know about how the process started and how the data were input in the system. After a while, the auditor asked her whether changes on the production lines that ensued were noted or not. She replied with a clear flash of anger, "How would I know what happens in manufacturing with these changes?"

Clearly, in this case the process owner couldn't explain the start and end of the process. And even worse, the auditor discovered that this person couldn't explain the start and end of the process because there was *no one* in charge of the engineering change process.

The auditor should follow the prioritized audit plan by targeting poorly performing processes as they relate to overall performance. When auditing a process, the auditor is trying to discern what's wrong with it and whether process performance is the cause of poor customer or overall performance. Next, the auditor performs process analysis using a turtle diagram and process characteristics to discern the process definition.

Audit Trails and Audit Planning. The prioritized audit plan has already considered the audit trails, including planning, performance evaluation, and improvement (PEI), risk and opportunity, new product development (NPD), and provision. The key to these audit trails is the choice of samples that the auditor follows. On the PEI audit trail, the auditor follows the links of internal/external issues and interested party expectations to objectives, processes, and the improvement plan. (See Chapter 2, Figures 2.6 and 2.8, for the Risk Sampling Sheet and Quality Objectives Sampling Sheet. Keep in mind that the auditor already has started this sample in Stage 1 of the audit.) The NPD audit trail samples "contracts" from sales, to new product development, to the product and process validation process. The provision audit trail follows the process flow of a part family using a process flowchart and an inspection sheet.

When the audit is being conducted, the auditor should follow side trails to investigate a problem. Remember, the auditor is focused on QMS performance, process performance, and customer satisfaction, including risk-based thinking. When the auditor is in the design department and an issue of training comes up, the auditor should follow that issue to the human resources department either then or later when the training process is audited. As another example, if while examining the "nonconforming product storage area" the auditor finds many samples noted as "design engineering samples" that have little or no identification, he or she is free to immediately follow this trail to the design department or note it for a later time.

Note that the audit shouldn't take place in a conference room but at the location of the auditee. Also, the auditor should audit the person or item being sampled while keeping in mind two issues: *relevancy* and *representative sampling*.

First, the sample taken has to be relevant within the scope of the ISO 9001 audit being conducted. This is an important topic of discussion for a third-party audit; for example, in an aerospace, defense, or space audit, an agricultural product being supplied by the auditee is not a good sample and is not relevant to the scope of the audit. In an internal audit, the scope is not as strict, and the auditor is free to pursue samples beneficial to the organization, unlike the third-party auditor. Relevancy in an internal audit may be more important in terms of keeping discipline with the samples taken for a particular audit topic. For example, when auditing management review, the internal auditor should stick to samples important to management review without suddenly jumping to design review or some other area. In other words, design review is not a relevant sample for the topic of management review.

The idea of representative sampling is important when auditing any area of the organization (for example, sampling purchase orders in purchasing). The auditor can randomly sample between steel suppliers A, B, C, and D, and chooses four purchase orders from each. However, in the audit this would be a nonconformity against the auditor. Why? The auditor didn't first understand the process. If the auditor had asked the right question, he or she would've found out that 80% of the steel is purchased from supplier D, 10% from A, and 5% each from C and D. Understanding this, the auditor should've selected samples based on the process.

The second application of representative sampling is in manufacturing. The auditor should ideally sample the key manufacturing processes as well as the product families key to the organization. See Chapter 2 for a discussion on sampling the production and service provision audit trail.

This same logic should be applied while sampling personnel within the organization. Top management should be audited for the PEI audit trail and processes. For all others, the process owners and those working in the processes should be sampled. The auditor should keep in mind the mix of personnel working in the organization and what the statistical breakdown is for top management, managers, engineers, quality, and workers on the plant floor.

Following the Prioritized Audit Plan. When conducting the ISO 9001:2015 audit, the priority is to determine whether the QMS is performing effectively. The QMS is defined as a set of interrelated or interacting elements that establishes policies, objectives, and processes to achieve these objectives. The auditor should sample personnel and records to also check conformance, that is, *shall*s, as well as ensure that each process is meeting its performance objectives. The auditor should complete each process audit keeping in mind that enough samples should be covered to verify that the process is implemented and that it conforms to the organization's process and is meeting its measuring and monitoring checks.

Links and Samples. As explained in stage 1, the auditor is required to prioritize the audit based on the organization's performance. Study examples of customer feedback, including nonconformity data, corrective action requests, results of satisfaction surveys, complaints regarding product quality, on-time delivery, service provision, or responsiveness to customers, and internal requests. Try to relate these failures to the processes that are not performing satisfactorily. The process map comes in handy when identifying which processes to sample.

Next, the auditor should complete a Process Analysis Worksheet, including a turtle diagram, to ensure that clause 4.4.1 requirements are being met. The key to an effective process analysis is to determine the actual inputs, outputs, and customer expectations. In the example already covered in this chapter and shown in Figure 4.3, inputs to the business reviews are the agenda items that will be covered during the meeting. The output is the action plan. Customer expectations for the outputs are fully attended meetings and actions. The expectations constitute the criteria or metrics/indicators to determine the effectiveness of the process.

Once this is done, the auditor should determine the methods and/or procedures, materials and/or equipment, and the competence, skills, and training required for the process to be effective. The process analysis or turtle diagram can be conducted prior to or in conjunction with the audit. It will show any weakness in the process definition.

Although the auditor has initiated the analysis during the stage 1 audit, he or she needs to interview the auditee (that is, process workers) to determine what's actually happening in the process (see Figure 4.4).

In the example in Figure 4.3, if the turtle diagram for management review showed a key problem identified from the performance analysis (for example, lack of actions), then this would be an area the auditor would explore further when conducting the audit. Questions based on the performance review and process analysis should be documented on the Process Analysis Worksheet prior to the audit, as discussed in step 8 of stage 1. During the audit, these questions should become the focus of the review of the effectiveness of the process. In other words, process performance and effectiveness should be the focus of the Process Analysis Worksheet.

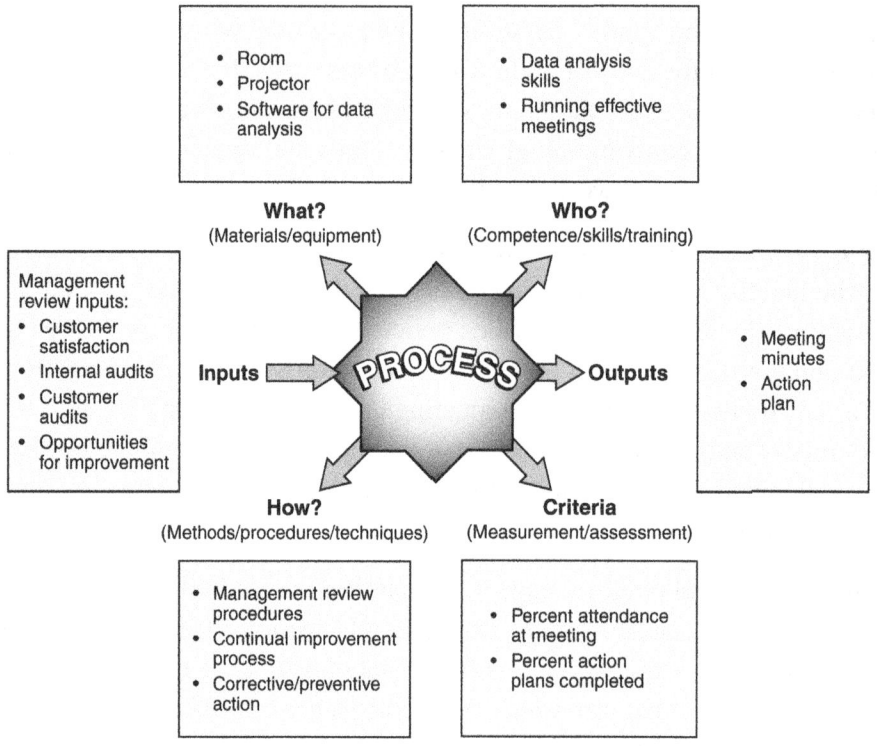

Figure 4.3 Turtle diagram—example of management review.

Completing the Process Analysis Worksheet. A Process Analysis Worksheet such as the one shown in Figure 4.5 should be used to record the objective evidence identified during the performance effectiveness auditing. One of the key areas of the worksheet is ensuring that process characteristics of a process have been addressed.

It's a good idea to complete as much of the Process Analysis Worksheet (See Figure 4.5) as possible for processes found to have performance issues prior to the audit. This includes thinking out the questions that need to be asked. When a suspect or poorly performing process has been identified, the organizational or customer performance issue should become the auditor's primary focus.

C.1 Conduct Facility Tour, If Needed

Step C.1, the facility tour, can be conducted as necessary by an internal auditor visiting from another location, or a second-party or third-party auditor when visiting a site or remote location for the first time (see Figure 4.1). Sometimes, a facility tour can be quite revealing. For example, I completed the opening meeting in a plant that claimed it wasn't responsible for design. During the plant tour, I was casually shown a small design group for a part going to a second-tier customer. For whatever reason, the plant had forgotten to mention this function at this site.

The plant tour can be used to confirm the information provided by the organization and the audit plan organized by the lead auditor. Sometimes, issues affecting the audit surface during

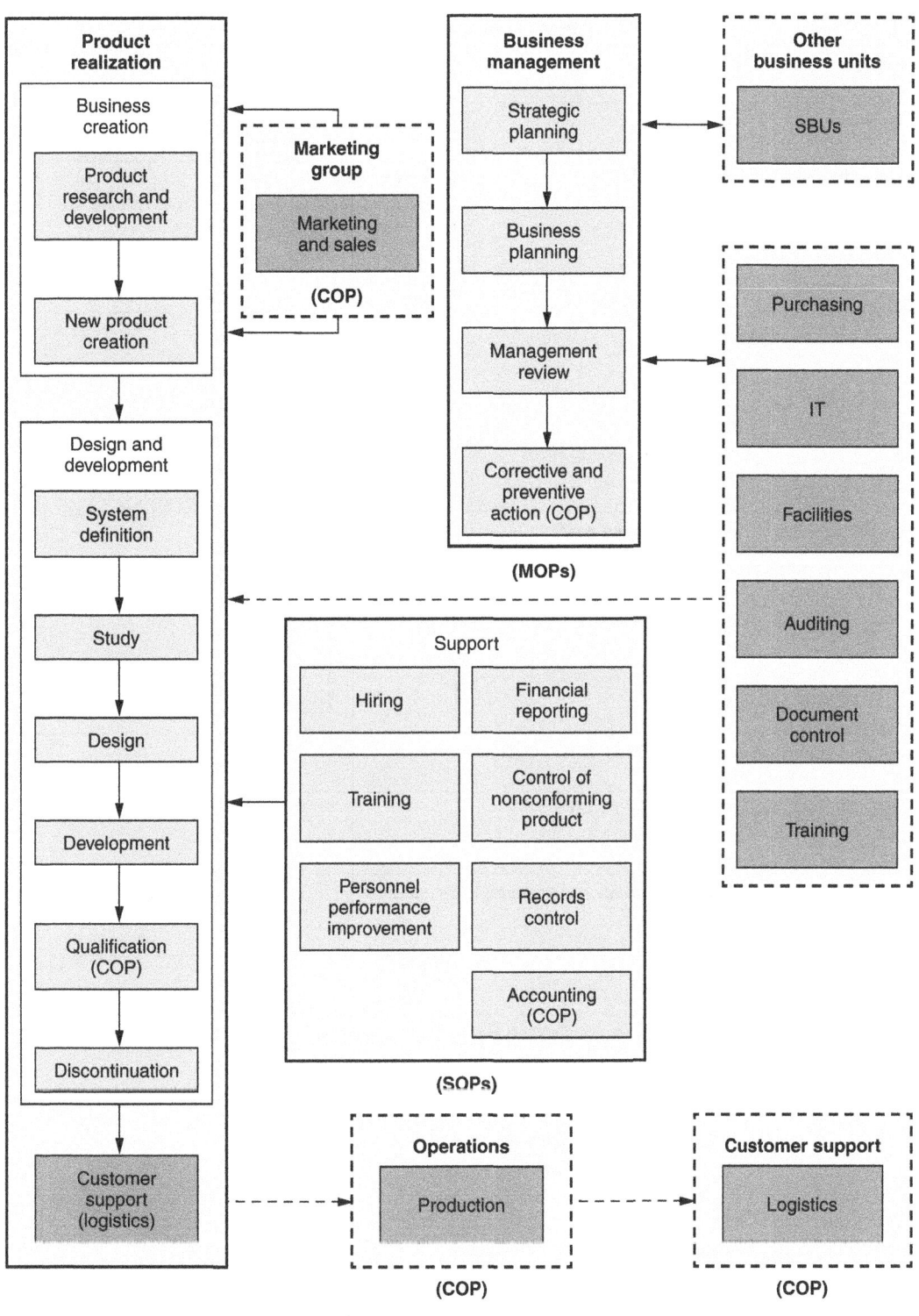

Figure 4.4 Process map example.

66 Chapter Four

Process Analysis Worksheet			
Company name:	Location:	Audit type:	Standard:
Auditor name:		Process:	
Reponsibilities/Process owner (clause 4.4.1e)		Process linkages (Predecessor) Subsequent process (clause 4.4.1b)	
Applicable clauses: Related quality objective or QMS performance metric:			
Related risk and opportunities analysis: ❏ Yes ❏ Not applicable			
Are the actions implemented? ❏ Yes ❏ No Explain:			
Is the organization meeting process performance indicators? ❏ Yes ❏ No			
If no, are there planned changes? ❏ Yes ❏ No			
Are the changes effective? That is, is the process showing improvement? Explain:			
Objective evidence: (What was sampled?)		Objective evidence: Customer-specific requirements applicable:	

Figure 4.5   Process analysis worksheet.

the tour. It's a good idea to hold a caucus meeting after the tour to discuss what each auditor saw and how it's going to be handled.

Auditor Requirements. Auditor requirements for step C.1 include the following:

- Modify the audit plan based on information collected during the opening meeting and facility tour
- Identify the need for translators, if necessary
- Write down issues or areas to investigate on the process worksheets

C.2 Study Customer and Organizational Performance

There may be up to 30 days or more between the stage 1 and on-site audits. During the interim, the auditor needs to reexamine the customer satisfaction scorecards and organizational performance, per step C.2 (see Figure 4.1).

Auditor Requirements. Auditor requirements for step C.2 include the following:

- Reexamine the customer scorecard. Has performance maintained the same level, or has it deteriorated?
- Study the last business performance review. Has the same level of performance been sustained? Did the organization follow up on the actions identified from the management review conducted during the readiness review?
- Has the organization been put on a customer-specific organizational approval status notification?
- Consider whether to adjust or reprioritize the audit plan based on the latest customer and performance issues.

C.3 Meeting with Top Management

Step C.3, the meeting with top management, includes a number of obligations from clause 5.1, Leadership and Commitment, in ISO 9001:2015, and clause 9.3, Management Review.

Auditor Requirements. As discussed earlier, top management's responsibilities are key to a successful QMS implementation. Moreover, ISO 9001:2015 has specific requirements for top management to fulfill. This audit of top management should take place within the context of the processes for the PEI audit trail.

Interview top management to learn the following:

- Alignment of the context, interested party expectations, quality policy, objectives, and *compatibility* with the strategic direction of the organization.
- *Integration* of the QMS with the business processes. In other words, there is only one set of processes running the organization.

- Understanding and *promotion* of risk-based thinking and the process approach.

- What the QMS *intended results* are and whether the organization is meeting them.

- Understanding of customer expectations and customer satisfaction and steps taken to improve customer satisfaction.

- Involvement in establishing, implementing, and maintaining the quality policy

- Understanding of customer and regulatory requirements and whether the organization is in compliance (*consistently met*). How do they track the requirements? What is the process for understanding and meeting them?

- Whether top management is taking ownership of the effectiveness of the management system. Whether they are taking an active role in working with subordinates (*engaging, directing and supporting*) and/or others in ensuring *effectiveness*.

- *Supporting* other managers in performing their responsibilities, that is, *demonstration* of leadership.

- Review of the quality management system at a periodic frequency to assess the "*suitability, adequacy, effectiveness, and alignment*" with the organization's overall "*strategic direction.*"

- Role in assigning specific roles and responsibilities as required (see clause 5.3).

The points above directly relate to clauses 5.0, Leadership, and 9.3, Management Review. Not understanding what the standard means and/or top management delegating responsibilities to others could very well result in a nonconformance for top management.

Overall, do the interactions with top management show a good understanding of the QMS and its performance? Is top management "accountable" for the effectiveness of the QMS?

Management Responsibilities That Can Be Delegated. Certain top management activities can be delegated, and some can't. When the word "ensure" is used in ISO 9001:2015, as in clause 5.1, Leadership and Commitment, those items can be delegated.

After the interview, determine how well the top manager answered the relevant questions asked regarding the QMS and its performance, alignment of the QMS with strategic direction, process performance, customer satisfaction, and risk-based thinking. Is top management playing their part for the success of the QMS and supporting their subordinates to ensure overall success of the QMS?

The auditor is asked to document his or her observations and record them.

C.4 Audit Organizational Processes

Auditor Requirements. Auditor requirements for step C.4 are as follows:

- When auditing a process, focus on the performance issues (if applicable) from stage 1 (see Chapter 3).

- Use an audit checklist and Process Analysis Worksheets as primary tools for auditing processes.

- Customize the checklist with issues that affect the customer or customer-specific QMS requirements, and/or appear to be poor process definition issues.

- Use the audit plan and the organization's defined processes, including sequence and interaction. Don't be requirements-oriented; be process-oriented.

- Be able to determine whether the organization is operating according to its process definition (that is, a process map and its sequence and interactions and documented information).

- Audit processes to determine whether each one is capable of meeting the key process indicators and is performing satisfactorily.

- Make sure that the customer-specific quality management system requirements are identified, addressed, and maintained in the business management system. (Note: Customer-specific requirements should be integrated into the processes.)

- Conduct interviews about the process with those that are involved in the process, at its location. Avoid conference room audits. When interviewing auditees, always take samples or have them show objective evidence to confirm their statements. The auditor should always choose the samples to avoid biased samples being given.

- Document both conformity and nonconformity in the Process Audit Worksheet. The information should be clear enough for an independent review by a third party, if necessary.

- Continue the audit trails from stage 1 for context and interested party expectations and risk processes. Use the same sampling sheets started in stage 1 (see Figure 4.6). For more on this audit trail see Chapter 2.

In Figure 4.7, the same quality objectives as above are reviewed for their plan, how they are deployed within the organization, and whether the management review shows evidence that the objectives are being met.

C.5 Verify That All Processes and Clauses Are Audited

The auditor should follow the audit plan and ensure that the audit encompasses all processes and clauses. Complete Figure C.6, documentation and process cross-reference for ISO 9001:2015.

D. Write Up Nonconformities

Nonconformities should be written during the audit as it progresses. Also, any nonconformities should be communicated to the auditee each day as findings.

Chapter Four

Risk Sampling Sheet					
Related interested party expectations* and internal/external issues (4.1 and 4.2)	Objectives and/or intended results (6.1.1)	Related risk and opportunities (6.1.1)	Plan to address risk and opportunities (6.1.2)	Related processes (6.1.2)	Evidence of actions implemented and effectiveness tracked (9.3.2)

*Note: Which internal and external issues and expectations are key to the organization? Has the organization adequately handled these expectations and issues when they set the objectives or "intended results"?

Figure 4.6 Risk sampling sheet.

Quality Objectives Sampling Sheet			
Quality objectives	Plan for meeting objectives (what will be done, resources, who is responsible, when it will be completed, how results will be evaluated) (6.2.1)	Deployed objectives (sample department and identify deployed objectives)	Objective evidence of objectives being met and actions completed (9.3.2)

*Quality objectives relate to the needs and expectations of interested parties and could result in objectives related to product quality, on-time delivery, or other expectations critical to an interested party, including customers. Note: Clause 6.2.1 requires quality objectives to be consistent with quality policy, be measurable, satisfy requirements, be relevant to products/services and customer satisfaction, and be monitored, communicated, and updated.

Figure 4.7 Quality objectives sampling sheet.

Nonconformities are a starting point for continual improvement, and as such are an important part of the audit. Auditors feel apologetic about nonconformities. They feel bad about finding issues with the organization's processes. This can cause auditors to avoid fundamental issues. For example, an organization that's conducting a management review only once a year is probably doing so only to satisfy ISO 9001:2015 rather than using it as part of its actual improvement process. A second company might not be following its own new product development process. A third company could be doing a poor job solving problems. The auditor should give each of these organizations a major nonconformity. Auditors should ask themselves whether they avoid giving nonconformities due to a lack of knowledge or reluctance to confront challenging organizational issues.

Another key structural issue noted by auditors is *interested party expectations and customer satisfaction*. Many organizations might not be interested party/customer-focused for any of the following reasons:

- The process does not capture interfaces with interested parties, including customers. Also, it does not show how data are collected, analyzed, and presented to top management so that they can take actions to become more interested party or customer focused.

- Setting of objectives isn't clearly linked to interested party needs and expectations.

- There are no clear actions or analysis of customer perception and scorecards designed to effectively address customer satisfaction or dissatisfaction.

Overall, auditors need to understand that organizations perform in a competitive and complex world. The seven audit trails, especially the PEI, NPD, and provision audit trails, really need to be effective. If they're not, the auditor simply must write nonconformities.

Major and minor nonconformities can be defined as follows.

Major nonconformity:

- A nonfulfillment of a requirement that is likely to result in the failure of a quality management system or reduce its ability to assure controlled processes or compliant products/services; it can be one or more of the following situations:

  – The failure of or total breakdown of a system in meeting an ISO 9001:2015 standard requirement, an organization procedure, or customer quality management system requirement

  – Any nonconformity that would result in the probable shipment of nonconforming product

  – A condition that could result in the failure or reduce the usability of a product or service for its intended purpose

  – A number of minor nonconformities against one process or related processes that may cause a system failure

Minor nonconformity:

- A nonfulfillment of a requirement that is not likely to result in the failure of a quality management system or reduce its ability to assure controlled processes or compliant products/services; it can be either one of the following situations:
  - A single system failure or lapse in conformance with an ISO 9001:2015 series standard or customer quality management system requirement
  - A single system failure or lapse in conformance with a procedure associated with the organization's quality management system.

All nonconformities need to be recorded but not closed during the audit. The internal auditor and the organization need to require the auditee to submit root cause analysis and evidence of systemic corrective action for each nonconformity issued.

A written nonconformity must include three items:

- Statement of nonconformity (system level)
- The requirement that's not being fulfilled
- Objective evidence

The statement of nonconformity is expressed as an issue with the system and shouldn't be expressed against a person or an incident. The nonconformity statement should define *the system problem.*

The unmet requirement should be quoted. It can be from ISO 9001:2015, the customer-specific requirements, and/or documentation of the organization. Auditors should carefully study the requirements of the ISO 9001 series standard being audited, or the organization's own processes that are being violated, and quote the section not being addressed. In no case should the auditor cite several clauses or many procedure numbers in a single nonconformity. Such a lack of precision from the auditor creates confusion for both the auditor and auditee.

The objective evidence and statement of nonconformity can be written in one or two sentences, maximum. Often, writing a paragraph doesn't make the nonconformity any more clear; it actually makes it more vague.

Auditors should be bold and have confidence in their abilities. They need to evaluate whether the process is working for the organization. Is the company satisfying its customers and market?

Auditor Requirements

- A written nonconformity must contain a statement of nonconformity with the system, the unmet standard requirement, and the objective evidence.
  - One nonconformity can be written to cover more than one "shall."
- Nonconformities must be categorized as major or minor (see definition above).
- Nonconformities should be cross-referenced to an organization's QMS and/or the relevant clause of ISO 9001:2015.

- Identify opportunities for recommendations without offering solutions.
- Use a format that has root cause, corrective action, and systemic action.

E. Closing Meeting

The auditor is responsible for three things during step E, the closing/closeout meeting:

- Determine audit team recommendations
- Prepare draft report
- Conduct the closing meeting

Auditors should be careful not to accept any nonconformity closeouts during the audit. Why? The organization will likely just fix the symptom instead of identifying the root cause and *then* fixing the problem. Can the organization actually implement a significant preventive action, or will this problem repeat again soon? It will probably repeat.

During the closeout, let the auditee know the deadlines for when the corrective action responses are needed.

E.1 Determine Audit Team Recommendations

Once all of the nonconformities are written, step E.1 a focuses on the audit team's recommendations. There are four outcomes:

- Minor and major nonconformities are so numerous that another system audit will be recommended to management.
- Minor nonconformities that can be closed via written documentation.
- Minor nonconformities that require on-site closeout.
- Major nonconformities that require on-site closeout.

E.2 Prepare the Draft Report

The minimum content for a draft report is all the nonconformities and the audit team summary. This draft report should be presented during the closing meeting and left with the auditee (see step E.2 in Figure 4.1).

Auditor Requirements

- Prepare draft reports describing all nonconformities. Also, identify and include the audit team summary, at a minimum.
- Identify nonconformities and opportunities for improvement. No other categories are allowed.

E.3 Conduct the Closing Meeting

Auditor Requirements. During step E.3, the closing meeting, the auditor has three responsibilities:

- Conduct the closing meeting using the closing meeting agenda (see below)
- Deliver the draft audit report
- Record any problems

Depending on the quality of the data provided, auditors shouldn't shy away from asking for objective evidence and physical closeouts. Internal audit systems should also define their corrective action submission timelines. (There will be more discussion of closeout requirements in section G.)

It's also a good idea to have an appeals process for internal and supplier audits similar to that of third-party registrar requirements. The appeals process should begin with the lead auditor and move up to a designated senior management person at the organization.

A typical closing meeting agenda includes the following:

- Statement of thanks
- Attendance list
- Scope, objectives, and criteria
- Significance of audit sample
- Audit standard, rules, and reference manuals
- Audit summary
- Root cause and systemic corrective action responses
- Opportunities for improvement
- Clarification of nonconformity statements and summary
- Statement of confidentiality
- Appeals process
- Follow-up
- Close

F. Audit Report

Step F, the audit report, includes requirements from ISO 9001:2015.

The audit report should include:

- Details of the auditee and the auditors.
  - Names of both parties.
  - Date and address at which the audit was conducted.
- Audit scope and products.
- List of customers and customer-specific quality management system requirements with revision level.
- Summary of the audit:
  - Good systems and/or processes found during the audit
  - Overall conclusion of the audit (for example, 14 nonconformities with two major nonconformities)
  - Systems and/or processes not working well that need to be improved
  - Positive feedback about the organization that may encourage them as they move forward
- Nonconformity summary. This is a detailed summary of the nonconformities identified by topic area, area found in, and so on. It's easier to see patterns when this list is analyzed.
- Objective evidence collected. The auditor lists all the evidence sampled for all the processes in the area.
- Attendance lists for the opening and closing meetings should be included. It's important that top management participates so that the audit will be perceived as truly value-added to the organization.
- Audit plans. These list all the details of the processes targeted and the persons interviewed.
- Clause-to-process cross-referenccs.
- Nonconformities. The audit report will provide all the nonconformities, identified sheet by sheet.

Formality of the Audit Report. The same type of formal report as in a third-party audit should be used for the internal audit. Formality in the audit and the audit report will help the internal audit be treated in the same manner as an external audit. Formality will also give the nonconformities and the closeout a sense of appropriate seriousness.

Documentation and Process Cross-Reference. The auditor should verify that the organization's processes cover all the requirements of the ISO 9001:2015 standard being audited. Clauses or sub-clauses not audited signify an incomplete system audit.

Management Representative Acceptance of Audit Report. It's good practice to have a sign-off from the organization's management representative.

Auditor Requirements

- Use the audit report model outlined in this chapter and shown in Appendix C
- Get sign-off from the auditee that he or she received the report

G. Corrective Action and Closeouts

Step G is the final and most important step of the audit (see Figure 4.1). It's also the only one where the organization being audited saves money. How does this happen? The savings occur when the auditor identifies customer and performance issues in the organization. The auditor subsequently traces the problem to suspect processes, which are then investigated during the stage 2 audit.

During the investigation, nonconformities are identified for process-related problems or lack of process performance that leads to customer and overall performance issues. For instance, during a recent audit an overall yield issue was traced to process issues in the organization. The plant manager told the auditors that this was the best audit in which he'd participated. He said that the issues identified were important to him and his overall success.

Depending on the issues, when an organization fixes the nonconformities identified by the audit, customer satisfaction will increase, and performance problems will be solved. Identifying problems during the closing meeting and in the audit report isn't enough, though. The organization's overall response to audit corrective actions must be effective, and the nonconformance must be closed out. Thus, it's helpful for the organization if the auditor identifies the process involved and the audit expectations.

The corrective action and closeout phase consists of two steps with different responsible parties. Corrective action is the responsibility of the auditee, and closeout is the responsibility of the auditor.

Auditee's Responsibility. For the corrective action step, the management representative usually assigns the corrective action to the process owner or the manager of a particular department. The first step the manager needs to take is to investigate the problem further and identify its true extent.

Let's say, for example, that two gages are found by an auditor to be out of calibration. The manager or process owner needs to investigate how many other gages are out of calibration. ISO 19011:2002 and ISO 9001:2015 require the manager or process owner to find the root cause and conduct the corrective action. The organization needs to go further and identify the system corrective action or preventive action. In other words, could the gage calibration problem occur in other departments, in other products, and/or in other plants? How did this problem occur in the first place, and how can the organization stop the problem from happening again? This, then, is one of the best practices recommended in this book for internal audits in the corrective action and closeout steps.

Auditor's Responsibility. The auditor should conduct follow-up verification to close out the nonconformity. He or she should first ask what the problem is, what the root cause related to the problem is, and whether the corrective action is related to the problem. Did the organization investigate the full extent of the problem? Did it determine the systemic root cause? If this first step is OK, the auditor should check to see that the corrective actions taken are implemented effectively. In Figure 4.8, the auditor checks to see if both of the corrective actions are implemented as stated.

Auditor

Statement of nonconformity (express as a system problem):

The problem identification system isn't working.
7.5.3 "The organization shall identify the product by suitable means throughout . . ."
—Auditor note

Objective evidence:

Three tubs of parts weren't identified with a product tag in department 350.—Auditor note

Auditee:

Extent of problem:

Spot audits were done by manufacturing personnel on all shifts during the week of 11/15/20XX, and they noted problems in many other departments, including 350, 340, 220, and 150.—Auditee note

Containment:

Immediately asked all departments, including 350, to tag all the untagged baskets. 11/16/20XX.—Auditee note

System root cause (use five whys, if applicable):

Operators aren't following tagging procedure. Some supervisors aren't stepping up and informing workers about the need to follow tagging procedures.—Auditee note
- Why? New employees and supervisors—Auditee note
- Why? Tagging isn't included in the new employee orientation training.—Auditee note

System corrective action and impact (auditee notes):

1. Train all plant supervisors on the tagging procedure, and ensure that they train operators who work in their departments. 11/30/20XX—J. Black
2. Conduct two manufacturing process audits a month. The process audits will survey many departments for tagging issues. Change implemented 11/30/20XX—M. Hank
3. Update new employee orientation training to include tagging by 11/15/20XX—D. Barnes

Auditor Closeout

Verification of corrective action (auditee notes):

- Reviewed training record 10-B for supervisory training held on 12/12/20XX. OK.
- Reviewed process audits for 11/20XX and 12/20XX. Is implemented and working.
- New employee orientation training updated. Verified 1/15/20XX.

Resample problem:

Reviewed tagging in departments 110, 315, 350 on 1/15/20XX. OK—Auditor note

---

Figure 4.8 Sample evidence of corrective action closeout.

The auditor needs to record objective evidence that the corrective actions, both containment and system actions, have been carried out. Lastly, the auditor needs to resample the problem to ensure that the problem went away.

G.1 Evaluate Root Cause Analysis and Systemic Corrective Action

During step G.1, the audit team turns its attention to root causes. There's a cause-and-effect relationship between a root cause and a problem (see Figure 4.9). The root cause can turn on the problem when it's present, and it can turn off the problem when it's removed. The team could use brainstorming or is/is not analysis (advanced tool used for problem solving) to identify the root causes. In most cases, there will be many root causes, but they all fall under one of the following three categories: an occur root cause, an escape root cause, and a system root cause. The *occur* root cause made the problem happen. The *escape* root cause allowed the system to let the problem escape. The *system* root cause allowed the problem to occur in the first place.

System Corrective Action versus Incident-Specific Corrective Action. If, for example, there were a nonconformity with two tubs not being tagged in department 350, the corrective action could be specific to that department, and the two tubs tagged. This would be called *incident-specific* corrective action.

System corrective action would look across the plant at the product identification process, or look at fixing the problem permanently in the system. For example, the product identification process would be fixed rather than just tagging the two tubs in department 350.

Corrective Action Formats Used in Industry. In 1995, there was a *corrective action report* (CAR) process widely used across industry. The format was fairly simple, with a problem column and two columns of short- and long-term corrective actions. These were followed by a column for the auditor closeout.

Omnex introduced the eight disciplines (8D) format for corrective action response in 1995 for audit closeouts. This is the most popular format used in industry. The "five whys" approach first introduced by Dr. Kaoru Ishikawa is a process of moving from the symptom to true root cause. Each time "why" is asked and answered, the true root cause becomes more apparent. Omnex also uses the advanced is/is not problem analysis tool that clarifies a problem, evaluates the effects of

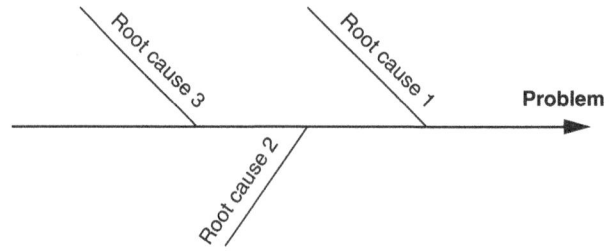

Figure 4.9 Root cause/problem relationship.

changes, and helps identify root causes. Both the five whys and is/is not analysis are covered with a number of other tools in the Omnex 8D class.

Sample Nonconformity and Corrective Action. Here's an example of how the seven-step process for problem resolution would be used on the "untagged tubs in department 350" problem referred to above. The auditor's responses are shown in italics.

1. Problem statement:

    Has the organization expressed the problem as a system issue? (Note: The specific incident identified in the problem isn't the system problem.)

    Yes, it has identified the system problem.

2. Containment action:

    Has the organization taken containment actions on the specific incidents cited by the audit team in its objective evidence? If external customers could be affected, then containment actions must be taken.

    It isn't known whether containment action was taken or whether the problem is indeed a risk to the customer. In other words, the tagging issue could end up as mixed parts. The answer is therefore not satisfactory.

3. System root cause:

    Has the organization found the root cause(s) of the problem in its system that allowed the incidents cited by the audit team to occur?

    Does the organization answer the question "What in our system failed that allowed this to happen?"

    Yes, the system root causes and five whys have been answered.

4. System corrective action and/or corrective action effect:

    Does the corrective action determined by the organization address changes to the system, not specific employees or machines?

    Does it address the root causes it has identified?

    Yes, it has identified corrective actions to the root causes identified.

5. Verification of corrective action:

    Has the audit team verified that the corrective action is implemented?

    - Major nonconformities need to have an on-site visit within 90 days of the end of the site audit.

- Minor nonconformities may require on-site verification within 90 days of the end of the site audit.

If not, include the verification in the audit plan for the next audit:

- The decision needs to be made by the auditor, that is, on-site verification or next audit verification.
- If the root cause can't be found, or if the corrective action can't be verified in 90 days, then the nonconformity should have an agreed-on action plan and containment.

Resampling of problem:

- The problem was resampled.

Auditor Requirements

- The auditor should study the nonconformity statement and the root causes associated with it. Do the root cause and the problem go hand in hand? Has the organization identified why the problem occurred and why the problem wasn't caught by the QMS? Blaming an operator or someone in the organization isn't an acceptable root cause.
- Study the corrective action associated with each root cause. Will it fix the problem in the system? Study the systemic corrective action. Can the system corrective action prevent the problem from recurring in the future?
- For each corrective action and system corrective action, sample incidents to verify that the action took place. Write the objective evidence in the closeout report.
- Sample the problem again to make sure it has been fixed. Why? Many times, root causes are just guesses at what caused a problem. The only real way the auditor knows the problem has been fixed is if it stops happening.

G.2 Complete a Follow-Up Audit as Needed

Step G.2 is concerned with the follow-up audit (see Figure 4.1)

Omnex recommends a follow-up audit only if there were major nonconformities and/or a number of minor nonconformities for internal audits.

Auditor Requirements. Sometimes, the closeout requires a follow-up audit because of a major nonconformity or risk to the customer, or simply because the closeout must be verified on-site.

There are several options available for closing out a nonconformity:

- The nonconformity can be closed out based on records. (This should be the choice of last resort for internal auditors due to their proximity to the audit location. This is only for minor nonconformities, *not* major nonconformities.)

- The nonconformity has paper evidence and a well-documented plan. The nonconformity can be closed out and rechecked in a subsequent follow-up audit. If there are a number of open issues based on records, the auditor should conduct an on-site audit within 90 days.

- The nonconformity poses a major risk to customers, so it requires on-site verification. However, it will take time to put the solution into place. In such a case, the auditor can do an on-site review of the containment actions and then revisit the scenario again during a surveillance audit or sooner.

CONCLUSION

This chapter provides guidance for completion of the stage 2 audit. The audit needs to be conducted in a specific way for it to be truly effective and satisfy all the ISO 9001:2015 auditing requirements. This chapter, along with the stage 1 guidance in Chapter 3, the ISO 9001:2015 audit checklist in Appendix D, and Process Analysis Worksheets, define the process for conducting the ISO 9001:2015 audit.

Conducting a monthly audit of a few processes and then calling it a system audit doesn't constitute a system audit. A *system audit* is a snapshot in time of how an overall system is performing. This includes all processes and all ISO 9001 clauses. Conducting monthly audits of a few clauses or processes at a time won't give the auditor a practical estimation of how the system is working as a whole.

Auditors are encouraged to develop their skills step by step. Becoming an effective auditor doesn't happen by taking one class or reading one book. It requires patience to develop the necessary knowledge and skills. Figure 4.10 shows the progression.

Risk management tools include:

- Understanding business process risk

- New product development process or advanced quality planning (AQP)

- Risk assessment, characteristics designation, and flow-down

- Design tools including system failure mode and effects analysis (SFMEA) and design failure mode and effects analysis (DFMEA) and associated tools

- Process tools including process flow, PFMEA, control plans, and work instructions

- Planning and conducting the PPAP or FAI

- Measurement systems analysis (GR&R, linearity, bias)

- Statistical process control (C_p, C_{pk}, and P_{pk}) capability indicators

For more information about the stage 2 audit, see the Confidential Assessment Report (Figure C.1).

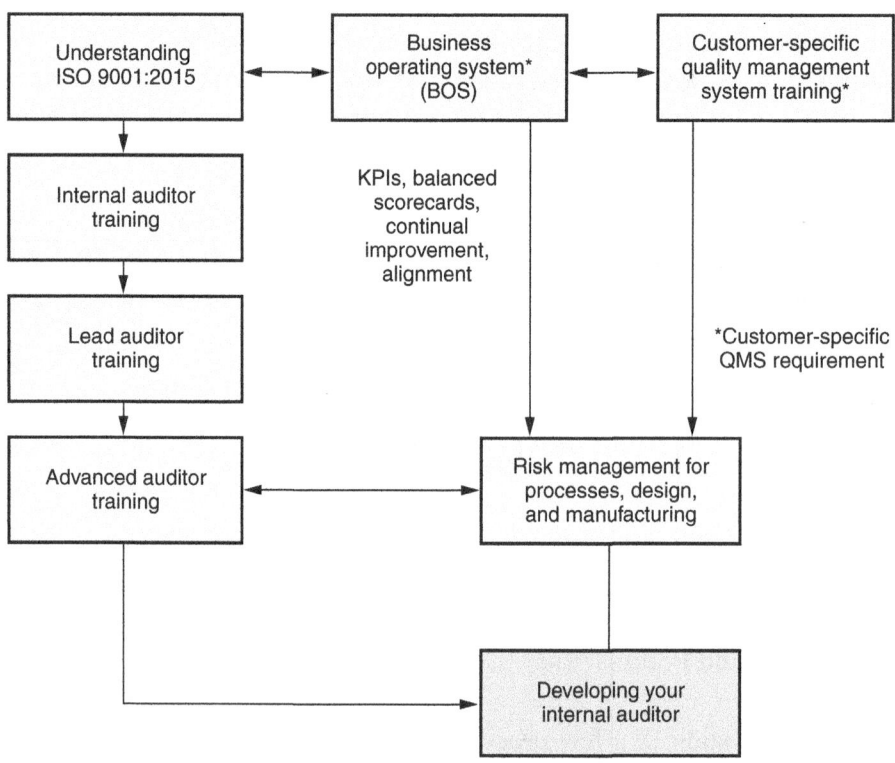

Figure 4.10 What makes a great internal auditor?

Appendix A

Introduction to Process Focus

UNDERSTANDING A PROCESS MAP AND PROCESSES

The process map is made up of process blocks that consist of groups of individual processes. For example, the product realization block would contain research and development, sales, product design, process design, manufacturing, and other related processes. To maintain this logical sequence, support process or management process blocks should be added to the process map. An important process in the management process block is how the organization conducts business strategy, objectives, and management review processes.

The process map should be limited to high-level processes that, in turn, may involve one or more other lower-level processes. Using the lexicon of level I—process map, level II—process flow, level III—work instructions, one can see a decomposition of process map blocks to processes to subprocesses. For example, the process of business planning may include the following procedures: gathering customer expectations, benchmarking, and setting and deploying objectives (see Figure A.1 for a sample process map).

ESSENTIAL PROCESS CHARACTERISTICS

When evaluating processes, here is what can be expected, from clause 4.4, Quality Management System and Its Processes (see Figure A.2):

- Does a process owner exist?
- Are there inputs and outputs defined for the process?
- Are there criteria, methods, and performance indicators to ensure effective operation and control?

84 Appendix A

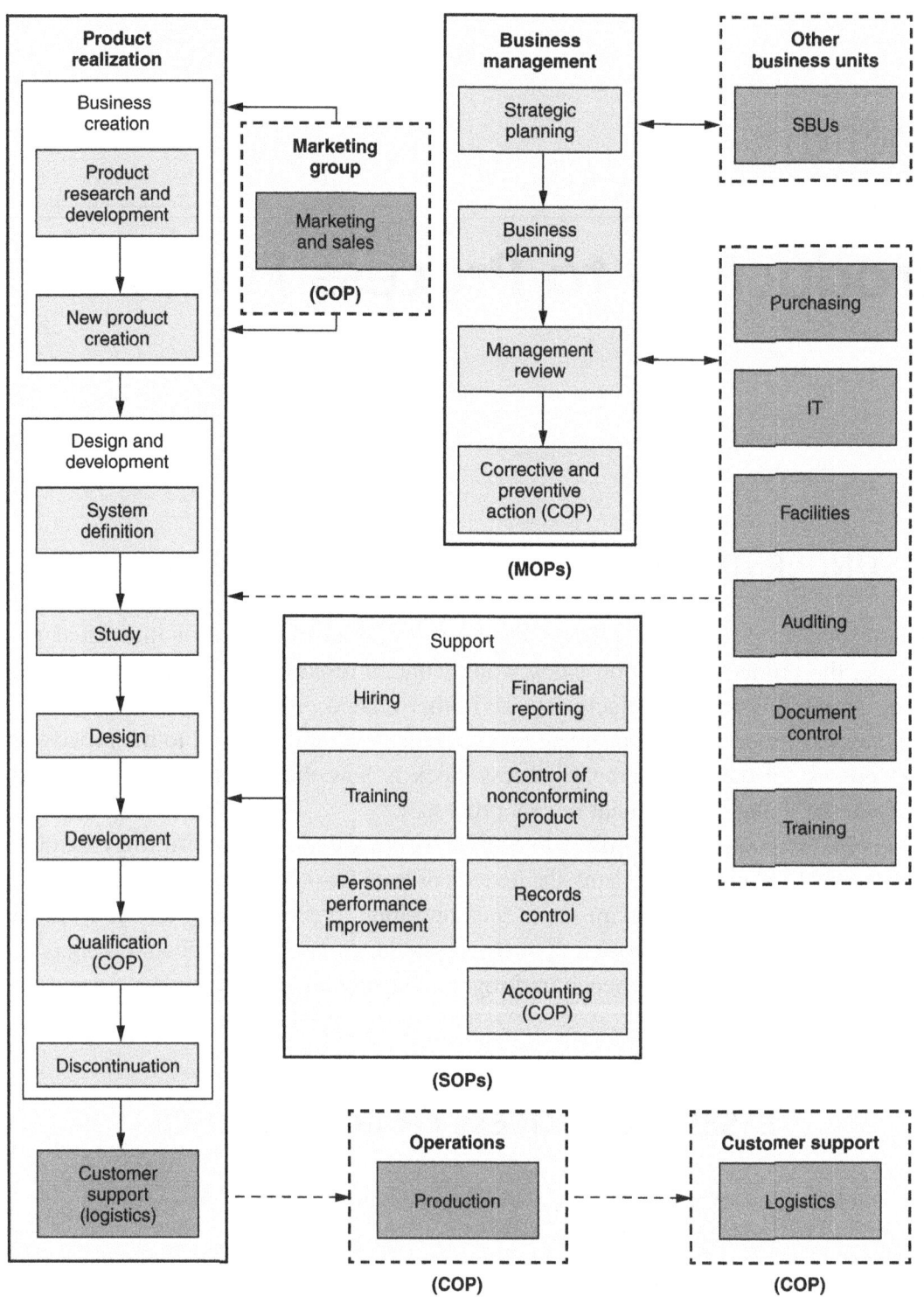

Figure A.1 Process map example.

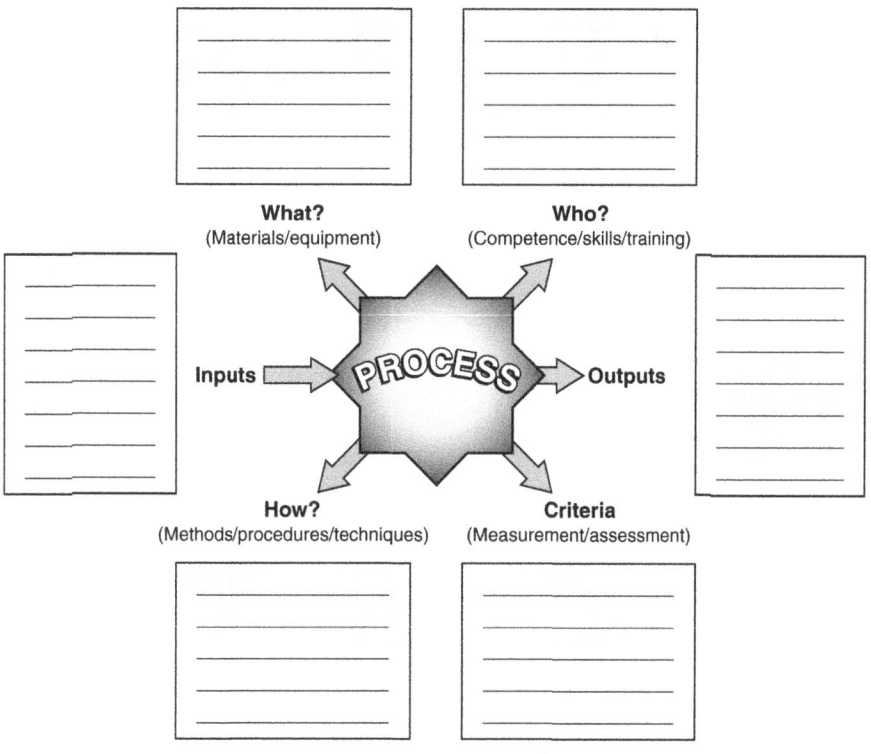

Figure A.2 Turtle diagram.

- Are there responsibilities and authority assigned? The expectation is a specific process owner.

- Are there risk and opportunities assigned as the process supports the "intended results" in the planning process?

- Are process links established?

- If the process does not achieve "intended results," are processes evaluated and changed?

- Is there documented information maintained to support the process?

- Is there retained documented information to ensure that processes are performing as planned?

PROCESS INTERFACES BETWEEN MANUFACTURING AND SUPPORT FUNCTION

The manufacturing site and support functions share processes and a flow of information between them. The "process interface" includes the links, communication, and information flows between the manufacturing site and a support function. Thus, when a sales process is studied at a corporate level, does it clearly show how it interacts with product design and the manufacturing plant?

The process map should illustrate the link between the manufacturing site and support function for many processes, including:

- Sales
- Purchasing
- Objectives deployment
- Management review data
- Management commitment
- Human resource planning
- Program management
- Advanced product quality planning (APQP) or new product development
- Customer complaints

The process map can't stop within the four walls of the remote location or the manufacturing site. It has to explain the flow of information and action between the site and the remote location.

PROCESS MAP AND PROCESS INTERFACES

Process interfaces are important not only between the site and remote location, but also between processes within the process map. For example, in the process map depicted in Figure A.1, the marketing and sales process links with product realization. What does that link mean in the actual process document? Does the process documentation that describes the sales and marketing process explain what type of information is exchanged between the two processes and define the input and output between the two processes? When one studies the product realization process, is the same information in the sales and marketing process shown as an input into the business planning process? This is what's meant by process interfaces—two processes, which are linked in the process map, that actually work together, as documented, in a real operation.

MEASURING AND MONITORING PROCESSES

A process-focused organization can explain and show how each process is measured, monitored, and improved. This organization will have not only a process map with process links between the main site and remote locations, but also evidence of process documentation, measurement, and monitoring, and an improvement plan. Process measurements must gauge the effectiveness and efficiency of a process and track performance for 12 months.

An organization must establish a process name, performance indicator, process champion, control method, process goal or objective, and means of tracking progress toward the goal or objective. If an organization isn't making progress, it needs to have an improvement plan. If necessary, changes need to be considered to achieve results.

RELATIONSHIP BETWEEN PROCESS PERFORMANCE AND OVERALL PERFORMANCE

After the auditor reviews the process map or its equivalent, he or she should study the sequence and interaction between overall QMS performance and process performance. For the sake of discussion, overall QMS performance will be called "results," and the measurement of results will be called KPIs, or *key performance indicators*. For example, if there's a problem in delivery, what processes are critical to helping the organization meet customer deliveries? The answer may be processes such as maintenance (which affects uptime), staffing (key jobs should be adequately staffed), and/or supplier management (that is, supplier parts availability). The auditor should be able to study the process data supplied and interview personnel during the stage 1 audit to ascertain suspect processes.

Processes help organizations achieve results. Processes can be improved; results are the result of processes performing. During planning (clause 6.0), risks and opportunities are analyzed and the actions that result are carved out by processes. These risks and opportunities associated with processes need to be determined and tracked for completion by the process owner.

AUDITING THE PROCESS FOCUS

Confirm Supporting Functions and Determine Audit Responsibilities and Results

Determine the Scope of the Audit. The auditor must begin by understanding the scope of the audit. This involves identifying the site, all its support functions, and all outsourced processes. The scope, products, and processes applicable to an ISO 9001:2015 audit should be fully established and studied. At this point, the auditor is asking questions to establish where the support functions are and how they're related.

Ask for Corporate Organizational Charts. Study all the locations and ask about each site and the different functions associated with it. Identify the site, its design function, purchasing profile (both direct and indirect), and top management. Next, identify all the sales offices. Identify warehouses and where lab testing takes place. These activities meet the requirements of auditing the site and its support functions. Through interviews, identify all outsourced processes (for example, product and/or process design, plating and/or heat-treating). Any process affecting product conformity that's performed for the organization by a supplier is considered an outsourced process. The auditor should identify each and ensure that these processes are included in the organization's QMS. The auditor should make a special note of outsourced processes and study the way the organization controls these processes during documentation review.

Identify Audit Responsibilities for the Site and Its Support Functions. Will one audit team be auditing the site, or are multiple auditors responsible? How will the process links and audit trail be managed? If there isn't an audit team responsible for the entire audit process, an agreement should be reached between the different auditors about handing off the auditing processes that connect the site to its support functions.

If only one audit team is responsible, then it will plan the sampling and auditing of processes that link the site and its support functions whether these are at the same site or at a remote location.

Processes Showing Sequence and Interaction

During the audit, the auditor should study the organization's process map or equivalent. Is the map location specific, and does it explain the processes in the organization being audited? As mentioned earlier, many processes connect between the site and remote locations. Business planning, objectives deployment, management reviews, new product development, purchasing, and sales are examples of processes that can overlap functional and/or geographical areas. Sample the process documents. Are the interfaces of the processes clearly identified between locations, or do the documents stop within the four walls of the site or support function? (See Figure A.3.)

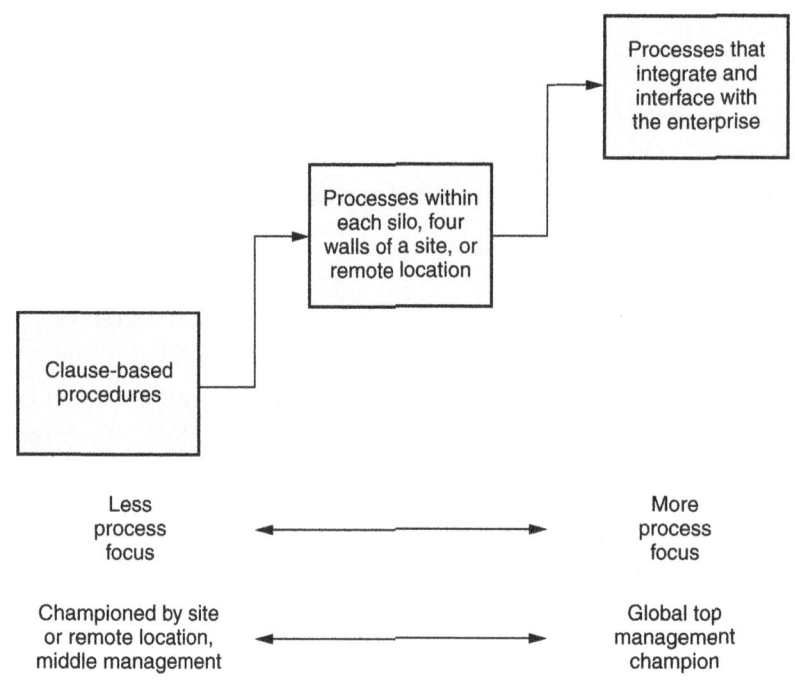

Figure A.3   Organization of processes by location.

Introduction to Process Focus   89

Study the Process Map

There are several other things to look for when studying the process map:

- It should be simple and at the same time descriptive enough to show the sequence and interaction.

- The processes depicted on the map can be meta-processes that flow into several lower-level processes typically documented in the level 2 procedures.

- Does the organization have a process map that shows how all the entities link together and how overall processes link corporate, sales, design, manufacturing, assembly, and the warehouse?

- Does the process map show the sequence and interaction of the processes at that site or entity?

- Study the links or process interfaces for multiple processes between the site and remote location as well as within the entity being audited. Do the inputs and outputs match? Does the process interface make sense relative to the process being studied? In Chapter 2, seven audit trails were introduced that will help the auditor evaluate links and samples that can check process interfaces.

- Be careful of process map paradigms, process versus clauses, and process versus functions. The auditor should be aware of a process approach versus a clause, departmental, or functional approach to developing processes. Processes identified by the organization shouldn't be repeats of the clauses in ISO 9001:2015. They also shouldn't be departmental or functional processes. Figure A.4 shows an elemental approach, and Figure A.5 shows a functional approach.

The process map shown in Figure A.4 is predominantly clause oriented. Its monitoring and measuring, resource management, PPAP, product realization, communication, internal audit, and data analysis elements are simply clauses of ISO 9001:2015. Furthermore, the process map shows no interactions and thus fails to document how the organization actually operates.

However, this map does illustrate the "quality paradigm" of professionals who have worked with standards. Many organizations have used procedures developed by quality professionals based on standards requirements from the 1980s. The quality paradigm makes it impossible for implementers or auditors to see beyond the requirements of standards to the processes that allow the organization to function.

Figure A.5 shows a process map that's based on the departments and functions of the plant. Instead of documenting processes, it shows the many departments in the plant, such as engineering, quality, information technology (IT), human resources, and production. Processes aren't functions or departments, but they do cut across them. This map also fails to indicate interactions between its various elements.

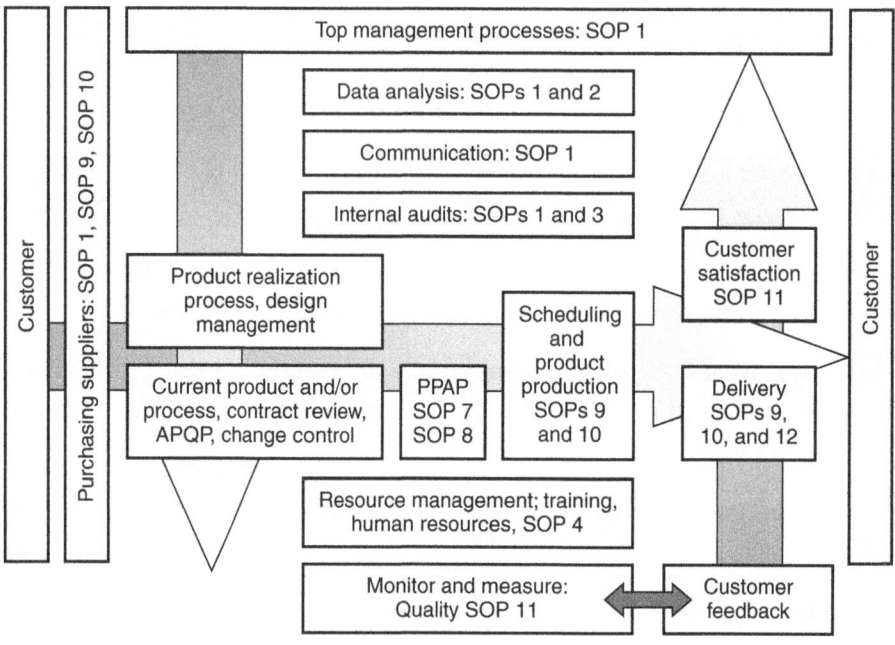

Figure A.4 Elemental approach.

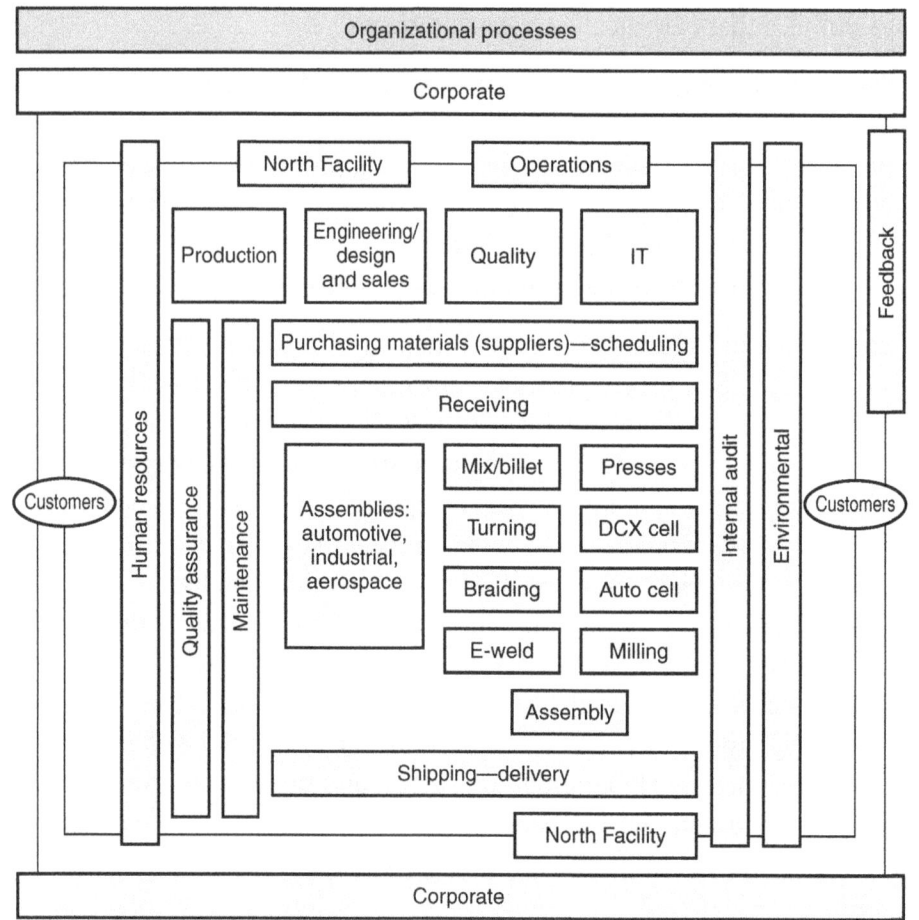

Figure A.5 Functional approach.

Appendix B

Assessment Report for Stage 1

Organization name: _____

City, State: _____

Organization contact: _____

Lead auditor: _____

CONTENTS

(See Chapter 3 for more details.)

1. Organization Information	92
2. Audit Plan—Stage 1	93
3. Opening and Closing Meetings Checklist—Stage 1	94
4. Obtain Materials for Stage 1 Readiness Review	94
5. Processes Showing Sequence and Interactions, Including Key Indicators	95
6. Conduct Documented Information Review and Confirm That Documented Processes Address All Requirements of ISO 9001:2015	96
7. Conduct Performance Analysis	100
8. Evaluate Internal Audits and Management Review Results	103
9. Identify Suspect Processes	106

10. Confirm Customer-Specific Quality Management System Requirements 106

11. Determine the Appropriate Scope. 107

12. Determine the Audit Feasibility 107

13. Create an Audit Plan. 108

14. Prepare and Deliver the Stage 1 Report 110

15. Conduct Process Analysis and Prepare Process Worksheet 111

1. ORGANIZATION INFORMATION

Organization name: _____

Contact person: _____

Department: _____

Telephone: _____

Fax: _____

E-mail: _____

Street: _____

City: _____

State or province: _____

Zip or postal code: _____

Standard: ISO 9001:2015

Type of assessment: Stage 1

Assessment team: _____

Person days: _____

Start date: _____

End date: _____

2. AUDIT PLAN—STAGE 1

Date	Time	Activity	Who	Comment for reader
	30 minutes	Opening meeting		
	1 hour	Facility tour (optional)		Not required for internal audits
	3 or more hours	Process approach and documented information review		Is the company process focused? Is there adequate documented information for the size and complexity of the business? Only performed typically in the first audit of a third-party audit. Subsequent audits will study documented information, but it will vary based on the audit.
	2 hours	Performance analysis—customer performance information (scorecards), business KPIs, customer complaints, process performance		Data are used to prioritize the audit and to understand performance issues related to the organization and its processes.
	2 or more hours	Management review, planning, and risks and opportunities, internal audits, and corrective action		Decision on whether to continue to stage 2 (feasibility of the audit) or postpone audit. Does the management system appear to be implemented and mature? Is the system mature enough to have "retained documented information" or records. In many instances, even though the auditee does not appear ready—for example, in an internal or second-party audit—the audit may need to proceed for continual improvement purposes. Due to cost considerations for travel, stage 1 and stage 2 audits may be held back to back. If stage 1 and stage 2 are held back to back, then some redundant stage 1 items may be skipped.
	3 or more hours	Audit planning and audit notes		Prioritize the audit based on the performance data, and also make notes on process weaknesses identified and areas that need to be investigated.
	30 minutes	Closing meeting		Closing meeting

Figure B.1 Audit plan—stage 1.

3. OPENING AND CLOSING MEETINGS CHECKLIST—STAGE 1

Opening and Closing Meetings Checklist	
Opening (process focus)/closing meeting. (Prepare and deliver the stage 1 report.) The client will maintain the original meeting attendance list and the original for each audit locally.	
Opening meeting discussion	**Closing meeting discussion**
❑ Introduce audit team and members	❑ Review scope
❑ Audit standard, rules, and reference manuals	❑ Audit standard, rules, and reference manuals
❑ Review scope and objective	❑ Audit methodology
❑ Confirm shift patterns and population	❑ Audit recommendations
❑ Confirm customer base (if applicable)	❑ Root cause and systemic corrective action response
❑ Review audit plan	❑ Confidentiality
❑ Audit methodology	❑ Appeal process
❑ Possible audit recommendations	
❑ Confidentiality of audit	
❑ Guides	
❑ Health and safety	
❑ Facilities review	
❑ Appeal process	
❑ Time and date for closing meeting	

Figure B.2 Opening and closing meetings checklist.

4. OBTAIN MATERIALS FOR STAGE 1 READINESS REVIEW

- Ensure that all of the required materials have been assembled and reviewed as required.
- Missing information and documents must be identified, and the organization must be apprised of them.

Required Materials

❑ Quality manual (if available)

❑ Description of processes showing the sequence and interactions, including the identification of any outsourced processes

❑ Performance measures and trends for the previous 12 months

❑ Documented information as per clause reference checklist

❑ List of documentation with decision level and revision date and annual schedule (gather last 12 months)

❑ Evidence of internal audits

- ❏ List of internal auditors and competency record, including management reviews retained for last 12 months

- ❏ The latest management review results

- ❏ List of all major customers

- ❏ Evidence of customer satisfaction and complaint summaries, including verification of customer reports, scorecards, and special status or equivalent

- ❏ List of customer-specific requirements

5. PROCESSES SHOWING SEQUENCE AND INTERACTIONS, INCLUDING KEY INDICATORS

Question: Has the organization provided a process description showing the sequence and interactions of processes?

❏ Yes

❏ No

Question: Are all the QMS processes documented? If not, how have they ensured processes are in control? Note: ISO 9001:2015 requires "documented information" to support the operation of processes, but this is not a requirement for documented procedures.

❏ Yes

❏ No

Question: Is process performance monitored for the processes sampled?

❏ Yes

❏ No

Study the process map. Ensure it is not clause and/or function focused and that it fully explains the organization, including the site and/or remote locations. Support processes could include business planning, new product development, purchasing, sales, and warehousing.

If there is a common process between the support location and the site, answer the following questions:

- Is process continuity maintained between the support location and the site?

- Are there two process owners or one?

- How is the process managed, measured, or improved?

- Is the shared process equally applicable to both the support location and the site?

- Do the outputs of the support process input directly to the site process and vice versa?
- If there are two processes—one for the support location and one for the site—are the inputs and outputs of each process clearly defined?

Note: The auditor must obtain a copy of the process description that shows all the interactions and attach it to the stage 1 audit report.

Study the links between processes and identify samples for the stage 2 audit. If the links are suspect, identify them in the Process Analysis Worksheet or in the Assessment Planning Table.

Classifications of Processes

The process description must show the interaction and sequencing of the organization's processes. The following is a partial list of possible processes.		
Customer-oriented processes (COPs)	**Support-oriented processes (SOPs)**	**Management-oriented processes (MOPs)**
Market analysis	Maintenance	Business planning
Bid/tender	Training	Management/business review
Order/request	Human resources	Internal auditing
Product/process verification/validation	Purchasing	Continual improvement
Manufacturing	Calibration	Analysis of data
Delivery	Laboratories	Customer satisfaction
Payment		Customer requirements gathering
Warranty service		Contract review
Post sale/customer feedback		
Note: ISO 9001:2015 does not classify processes as COPs, MOPs, or SOPs. Some sectors such as automotive and aerospace have elected for this classification.		

Figure B.3 Classifications of processes.

6. CONDUCT DOCUMENTED INFORMATION REVIEW AND CONFIRM THAT DOCUMENTED PROCESSES ADDRESS ALL REQUIREMENTS OF ISO 9001:2015

Use the documentation and process cross-reference for ISO 9001:2015 (Figure B.4) to document whether all the requirements, that is, *shalls*, are addressed in the process documents. Then use the document and process cross-reference completed by the auditee to understand what processes satisfy which clauses of the standard.

Complete the documentation and process cross-reference checklist. See Chapter 2 and the checklist for more guidance.

Documentation and Process Cross-Reference for ISO 9001:2015				
Clause	Clause heading	Organization's process number/description/ document reference[1,2]	Process owner[1]	Stage 1 result[3] (C-O-N/A)
4	Context of the organization			
4.1	Understanding the organization and its context			
4.2	Understanding the needs and expectations of interested parties			
4.3	Determining the scope of the quality management system			
4.4	Quality management system and its processes			
4.4.1	No Title			
4.4.2	No Title			
5	Leadership			
5.1	Leadership and commitment			
5.1.1	General			
5.1.2	Customer focus			
5.2	Policy			
5.2.1	Establishing the quality policy			
5.2.2	Communicating the quality policy			
5.3	Organizational roles, responsibilities and authorities			
6	Planning			
6.1	Actions to address risks and opportunities			
6.1.1	No Title			
6.1.2	No Title			
6.2	Quality objectives and planning to achieve them			
6.2.1	No Title			
6.2.2	No Title			
6.3	Planning of changes			
7	Support			
7.1	Resources			
7.1.1	General			
7.1.2	People			
7.1.3	Infrastructure			
7.1.4	Environment for the operation of processes			
7.1.5	Monitoring and measuring resources			
7.1.5.1	General			
7.1.5.2	Measurement traceability			
7.1.6	Organizational knowledge			
7.2	Competence			
7.3	Awareness			
7.4	Communication			
7.5	Documented information			

Figure B.4 Documentation and process cross-reference for ISO 9001:2015.

Documentation and Process Cross-Reference for ISO 9001:2015

Clause	Clause heading	Organization's process number/description/ document reference[1,2]	Process owner[1]	Stage 1 result[3] (C-O-N/A)
7.5.1	General			
7.5.2	Creating and updating			
7.5.3	Control of documented information			
7.5.3.1	No title			
7.5.3.2	No title			
8	Operation			
8.1	Operational planning and control			
8.2	Requirements for products and services			
8.2.1	Customer communication			
8.2.2	Determining the requirements for products and services			
8.2.3	Review of the requirements for products and services			
8.2.3.1	No title			
8.2.3.2	No title			
8.2.4	Changes to requirements for products and services			
8.3	Design and development of products and services			
8.3.1	General			
8.3.2	Design and development planning			
8.3.3	Design and development inputs			
8.3.4	Design and development controls			
8.3.5	Design and development outputs			
8.3.6	Design and development changes			
8.4	Control of externally provided processes, products and services			
8.4.1	General			
8.4.2	Type and extent of control			
8.4.3	Information for external providers			
8.5	Production and service provision			
8.5.1	Control of production and service provision			
8.5.2	Identification and traceability			
8.5.3	Property belonging to customers or external providers			
8.5.4	Preservation			
8.5.5	Post-delivery activities			
8.5.6	Control of changes			
8.6	Release of products and services			
8.7	Control of nonconforming outputs			
8.7.1	No title			
8.7.2	No title			
9	Performance evaluation			

Figure B.4 *Continued.*

Documentation and Process Cross-Reference for ISO 9001:2015				
Clause	Clause heading	Organization's process number/description/ document reference[1,2]	Process owner[1]	Stage 1 result[3] (C-O-N/A)
9.1.1	General			
9.1.2	Customer satisfaction			
9.1.3	Analysis and evaluation			
9.2	Internal audit			
9.2.1	No title			
9.2.2	No title			
9.3	Management review			
9.3.1	General			
9.3.2	Management review inputs			
9.3.3	Management review outputs			
10	Improvement			
10.1	General			
10.2	Nonconformity and corrective action			
10.2.1	No title			
10.2.2	No title			
10.3	Continual improvement			

Note 1: Shaded areas in light gray are to be completed by the organization (auditee); areas in the darker gray are to be completed by the auditor.

Note 2: Process numbers/descriptions/document references must be linked to the organization's (auditee's) process map.

Note 3: C refers to "conformance," O refers to "observations," and N/A stands for "not applicable."

C is in conformance for all documented processes if all the "shalls" are addressed in the documentation. Also, the processes need to include "who," "what," and "when."

Figure B.4 *Continued.*

Question: Do the processes documented address all the "shalls" of ISO 9001:2015?

❏ Yes

❏ No

If the answer is no, detail findings: _____

Question: Were samples taken from the documentation and process cross-reference matrix?

❏ Yes

❏ No

If the answer is yes, list the samples: _____

7. CONDUCT PERFORMANCE ANALYSIS

ISO 9001:2015 has performance expectations of the QMS in multiple areas of the standard, including for leadership in clause 5.1.1 and in planning in clause 6.1 for "intended results," and for QMS performance and effectiveness to be monitored, evaluated, and retained in clause 9.1, analyzed and evaluated in clause 9.1.3, reviewed in management review in clause 9.3, and improved in clauses 10.1 and 10.3.

Study the customer satisfaction (perception), customer satisfaction supplemental (scorecards), customer complaints and problem solving, and overall performance (or KPIs) of the organization. Poorly performing indicators or metrics represent lack of "intended results" or customer dissatisfaction for the organization, both requirements of clause 6, Planning, and clause 5.1.2, Customer Focus.

An ISO 9001 audit begins with the auditor analyzing overall customer satisfaction and organizational performance. Poorly performing indicators or lack of results are then linked by the auditor to poorly performing or suspect processes. They also could be indicators of poor risk analysis and/or implementation of actions in regard to risk and opportunities. These are documented in the Process Analysis Worksheet. The auditor also takes these results into consideration when auditing management review and/or process performance, and investigates how the organization responds when performance falls short.

Having no problems in customer metrics or customer scorecards does not necessarily mean high satisfaction. Bottom line, satisfaction can only be gauged by getting the customer's perception. This entails asking the customer some variant of the question, "Overall, how satisfied are you with us?"

Question: Have all customers, customer scorecards, and organizational performance issues been identified?

❏ Yes

❏ No

Question: Is there an overall process for gathering data in regard to interested party and customer needs and expectations? Does the process show interactions with interested parties? How are these data used for planning, and has the organization set customer-focused objectives?

❏ Yes

❏ No

Update Figure B.5 Information from scorecard. Also, update Figure B.6, Assessment Planning Table.

Question: Is there a prioritized list of interested party expectations?

❏ Yes

❏ No

Information from Customer Scorecard				
Customer	Customer quality performance	Customer/ assembly plant disruptions	Delivery schedule performance	Other

Figure B.5 Information from customer scorecard.

Assessment Planning Table	
Customer and performance issues	Related suspect processes

Figure B.6 Assessment planning table.

Identify top five interested party expectations in the Risk Sampling Sheet (Figure B.7).

Identify related issues as well.

Question: Are the "intended results" or objectives set based on the context and interested party expectations gathered?

❏ Yes

❏ No

Complete the "objectives and/or intended results" column in the Risk Sampling Sheet.

Question: Are there any open customer complaints?
❏ Yes
❏ No

Risk Sampling Sheet					
Related interested party expectations* and internal/external issues (4.1 and 4.2)	Objectives and/or intended results (6.1.1)	Related risk and opportunities (6.1.1)	Plan to address risk and opportunities (6.1.2)	Related processes (6.1.2)	Evidence of actions implemented and effectiveness tracked (9.3.2)

*Note: Which internal and external issues and expectations are key to the organization? Has the organization adequately handled these expectations and issues when they set the objectives or "intended results?"

Figure B.7 Risk sampling sheet.

Question: If yes, has a corrective action plan been implemented or proposed? (Note: Corrective action implemented or proposed should include root cause analysis followed by systemic corrective action.)

❏ Yes

❏ No

Review and analyze the 12 months of customer complaint history and document any trends, along with the related suspect processes, in the Assessment Planning Table (Figure B.6). Review the data for the following trends:

- Repeat issues
- Serious customer issues (for example, prism, yard hold, spills, or recalls)
- Blip or trend in performance

Review the organization's Pareto analysis for trends in departments, product families, manufacturing processes, or design issues.

8. EVALUATE INTERNAL AUDITS AND MANAGEMENT REVIEW RESULTS

Internal Audits

Internal audits are a good gauge of how well the organization understands itself. The auditor reviews the internal audit to ensure that the organization has conducted a complete system audit that includes all the organization's processes and all the clauses of ISO 9001:2015. The organization is expected to have 12 months of audit history, especially after the initial audit registration.

Audits should be scheduled based on status, importance, and the organization's annual plan. Also, the audits must be based on customer complaints, internal/external performance data, and how the internal audit has considered the customer-specific quality management system requirements.

Study the quality of the audit and the nonconformities issued. Does the internal audit include all the issues noticed in the organization thus far? Is the audit adequate? The nonconformities issued should have three parts: nonconformity, quote of the unmet requirement, and the objective evidence. What is the quality of the nonconformities; are they clear and concise?

Check out the quality of the nonconformity closeouts. Is there objective evidence to show that the corrective action has been implemented? Also, is there evidence that the system corrective actions have been implemented? Is there evidence to show that the problem will not repeat?

System Audit

System audits are conducted periodically (at minimum once a year) to provide top management a snapshot review of the quality management system. System audits should be conducted with the same formality as third-party audits and should use the same processes and time durations as an initial audit. System audits should cover all the process map processes and all the clauses in ISO 9001:2015. Note: System audits are not a series of short audits conducted monthly, but are a snapshot in time of the overall health and vitality of the QMS.

The intent of these audits is to ascertain whether the overall system is "effective and efficient." This is the formal audit, which needs to be conducted similarly to an external audit. In this audit, the auditors are ensuring that the organization is moving toward its goals and objectives and that customer satisfaction is showing happy customers.

Process Approach versus Clause or Elemental Approach

The audit must follow the process approach of the organization (see Appendix A). The audit plan must contain processes from the organization's process map. Processes aren't chosen randomly but are prioritized based on risks to the customer (for example, customer satisfaction, customer complaints, and organizational performance).

Overall Performance

The organization's overall performance must be gauged by examining records of management review. Note: Sometimes, auditees only conduct a management review once a year to comply with ISO 9001, and then only do it to show the records to the auditor. This type of "compliance" for such an important requirement should be duly recognized as a major nonconformity.

The management review must be conducted at suitable intervals to assess overall improvements and to note whether the organization is meeting business objectives and satisfying its customer needs and expectations. It is important for the auditor to note whether the management review is just a presentation of facts or a meeting that is improvement-oriented and evaluates the need for changes to the overall management system, quality policy, and objectives.

At a minimum, the management review or business review must cover these topics:

- Status of actions from previous management reviews

- Changes to external and internal issues (business context) that affect the quality management system

- Information on the performance and effectiveness of, and trends in:

  - Customer satisfaction and feedback from relevant interested parties

  - Quality objectives and whether they have been met

  - Process performance and product and service conformity

  - Nonconformities and corrective actions

  - Monitoring and measurement results (see clause 9.1.1; the organization needs to be explicit in what they monitor and measure, and the monitoring and measurement needs to evaluate the performance and effectiveness of the QMS)

  - Results of audits

  - Performance of external providers

The auditor shouldn't expect the organization to cover each topic during every business review. However, the topics must be covered according to top management requirements to move the organization forward. Also, it is important to evaluate the management review's output to ensure that it includes decisions and actions for improving the quality management system, changes to the QMS, and resource needs.

Overall performance should be gauged according to the "intended results" of the QMS (see clause 6.1.1a) and the quality objectives, and examining the business reviews that move the company forward on a weekly and monthly basis. Review the key indicators of the business, and note those that are performing poorly. Assess the overall quality of the business reviews. Is the company progressing toward its objectives? Also, do the objectives reflect customer/interested party needs, expectations, and key concerns?

Measuring Key Indicators and Performance Trends

Although it's not a requirement, the ISO 9001:2015 auditor expectation is that the organization will measure trends on a chart that shows variables on the Y-axis and time, typically in months, on the X-axis. Omnex recommends the use of trend charts, Pareto charts, and summaries of actions taken to improve a key indicator.

Question: Has a complete management review cycle been conducted that includes 12 months of records? The management meeting records should cover the minimum requirements of ISO 9001:2015; refer to clause 9.3.

❑ Yes

❑ No

Question: Is there output from the management review that's action and improvement oriented?

❑ Yes

❑ No

Question: Does the organization track performance, effectiveness, and trends as required in the management review? Performance indicator examples include internal ppm, yield, inventory turns, and availability.

❑ Yes

❑ No

Question: Are corrective action plans established for indicators that don't meet established goals? For those indicators not meeting the goals, document these indicators in the Assessment Planning Table (Figure B.6) along with the related suspect processes.

❑ Yes

❑ No

Question: Are the organizational objectives and goals consistent with the quality policy?

❑ Yes

❑ No

Question: Has a complete internal audit been conducted? (Review 12 months of internal audit history.) The internal audit should have been completed, covering all processes and clauses.

❑ Yes

❑ No

Question: Are all nonconformities resulting from the full system internal audit closed? Internal audit nonconformities shall be addressed through root cause analysis and systemic corrective action.

❏ Yes

❏ No

9. IDENTIFY SUSPECT PROCESSES

Based on the analysis of customer and performance data, identify poorly performing processes that affect overall performance. Using the Assessment Planning Table (Figure B.6), analyze the QMS performance issues, processes, customer scorecards, management review performance data, and customer complaints. What are the key performance issues?

Identify the suspect processes that affect performance. Use the process identified in the process map to identify the relationship between intended results and process performance. Prioritize the processes as they relate to product or process performance. Based on the analysis of the performance data, document processes that show weakness and require increased focus during the stage 2 audit.

An audit plan should be organized according to processes from the organization's process map, not by clauses in the standard. The audit plan should be prioritized according to "suspect" processes identified during customer focus and performance analysis. Next, the auditor should identify the sequence of processes to audit by referring to the audit trails discussed in Chapter 2. Study the process map and identify the planning, performance evaluation, and improvement (PEI), risk, new product development (NPD), and production and service provision (provision) audit trails.

10. CONFIRM CUSTOMER-SPECIFIC QUALITY MANAGEMENT SYSTEM REQUIREMENTS

Each on-site audit (that is, initial, surveillance, and recertification) shall include an audit of the organization's implementation of new customer-specific requirements since the last audit (see Figure B.6).

Question: Has the organization adequately defined its customers and the supplementary QMS requirements?

❏ Yes

❏ No

Question: Does the organization have a process to gather and update customer-specific quality management system requirements?

❏ Yes

❏ No

Question: Has the organization integrated customer-specific quality management system requirements into the QMS processes?

❏ Yes

❏ No

11. DETERMINE THE APPROPRIATE SCOPE

The scope is inherently linked to the process approach, and especially the *site* and the *remote location functions*. Customers and customer-specific quality management system requirements also affect the scope.

Question: Does the scope adequately reflect the organization's operation? When determining the scope, the requirements in ISO 9001:2015 clause 4.3 must be taken into account.

❏ Yes

❏ No

12. DETERMINE THE AUDIT FEASIBILITY

In third-party audits, the audit feasibility of the organization to proceed to stage 2 is determined. If the organization isn't ready to conduct the stage 2 site audit, the certification body and the organization can agree to stop the process.

In the internal audit or a supplier audit, this is really not a choice. If the organization is not ready, the internal auditors can issue nonconformances that can be added to the final audit report (see Figure B.9) or closed out during the stage 2 audit.

Stage 1 audit results shall be documented and communicated to the organization.

The stage 1 audit is the most critical step of the audit, so auditors should be thorough and provide nonconformities as necessary for improvement.

For guidance to internal auditors, the following situations typically may require postponement in a third-party situation, or a major nonconformity in an internal audit or supplier audit:

- Customer scorecards show that the organization is under a special status category. Some of the customer-specific organizational approval statuses include limited approval, probation, suspension, or withdrawal.

- The organization doesn't have one year of internal audits, management reviews, or performance data.

- An internal system audit to ISO 9001:2015 (all processes, clauses, or aerospace process approach to audits) hasn't been completed.

- Management review shows no top management involvement, or the management review is incomplete.

- The organization shows poor context, interested party expectations, or process focus.

- Documentation shows many requirements not being addressed by the organization's processes (documented or otherwise)

If there are obvious major nonconformities with respect to the implementation of the management system, and/or performance or customer issues, the auditor notes them and issues major nonconformities, or identifies them in the audit checklist for the stage 2 audit.

13. CREATE AN AUDIT PLAN

Creating a prioritized audit plan based on weaknesses in customer and organizational performance is a key to a good audit. Following the audit trails described in Chapter 2 is a good method for understanding linkages between processes and the ISO 9001 clauses, and for sample taking (see Figure B.8).

Study the organization's process map and identify the audit trails—PEI, new product development (NPD), and provision audit trails (see Chapter 2).

Stage 2 Audit Plan					
Objective: To verify conformance to ISO 9001:2015					
Date	Time	Auditor	Location	Organization's process #/description	Standard clauses
				Opening meeting	
				Facility tour	
				Review of customer scorecard and associated corrective action	

Figure B.8 Stage 2 audit plan.

- Audit the PEI processes and top management at the beginning of the audit. Identify objectives and their plans.

- Start with customer expectations, customer satisfaction, and customer scorecards. Obtain top management's thoughts and ideas on key issues from the customer's viewpoint.

- Identify which auditor is more proficient in each audit trail, and update the audit plan with the processes related to PEI, NPD, and provision audit trails.

- Identify all suspect processes and ensure they are in the audit plan.

- Complete Figure B.4, documentation and process cross-reference for ISO 9001:2015, and ensure that all clauses are being audited.

- Identify OEM and other customer-specific quality management system requirements and make notations in the audit plan to ensure that the customer-specific requirements will be sampled.

- Audit based on the defined processes of the organization and not the ISO 9001 clauses.

- Begin with an audit of top management and cover the following:

    - Areas of risk to the customer, including customer complaints and customer dissatisfaction.

    - Interested party expectations and key expectations affecting the organization.

    - Internal and external issues key to the organization.

    - Internal audits.

    - Management review and actions.

    - Progress toward continual improvement as related to set objectives.

    - Effectiveness of corrective actions as related to customer issues.

    - Leave time in the audit for the top management interview (see Chapter 3).

Finally, the auditor should keep in mind:

- Analysis of actual or potential risk to the customer, product, and processes.

- Demonstration of links between audit trails.

- Auditing manufacturing activities on all shifts where they occur.

- Optimizing audit time based on the organization's layout.

- Auditing support functions, with process links referenced planned on-site prior to the audit.

- Customer-specific quality management system requirements and all relevant processes, including new customers since the last audit.

- Customer concerns and/or complaints, special status notification, and the organization's response.

- Internal audit and management review results and actions.

- Progress made toward continual improvement.

- Effectiveness of corrective actions and verification since the last audit.

- QMS effectiveness with regard to achieving both customer and organizational objectives.

- Distributing the audit plan to the organization and all audit team members.

14. PREPARE AND DELIVER THE STAGE 1 AUDIT REPORT

Internal and supplier auditors can identify any major or minor nonconformities and report them in the internal audit (see Figure B.9).

Nonconformities identified during this stage 1 audit.	
NC #	**Nonconformity description**

Figure B.9 Stage 1—nonconformities.

15. CONDUCT PROCESS ANALYSIS AND PREPARE PROCESS ANALYSIS WORKSHEET

The auditor should use the Process Analysis Worksheet (Figure B.10) for auditing all processes. The process analysis allows the auditor to evaluate inputs, outputs, resources, measurement, monitoring, and methods. The performance analysis and process analysis should assist the auditor in the stage 1 audit to develop process-related questions in the process worksheet.

Process Analysis Worksheet			
Company name:	Location:	Audit type:	Standard:
Auditor name:		Process:	
Reponsibilities/Process owner (clause 4.4.1e)		Process linkages (Predecessor) Subsequent process (clause 4.4.1b)	
Applicable clauses: Related quality objective or QMS performance metric:		*Process diagram showing Inputs and Outputs with What? (Materials/equipment), Who? (Competence/skills/training), How? (Methods/procedures/techniques), Criteria (Measurement/assessment)*	
Related risk and opportunities analysis: ❏ Yes ❏ Not applicable			
Are the actions implemented? ❏ Yes ❏ No Explain:			
Is the organization meeting process performance indicators? ❏ Yes ❏ No			
If no, are there planned changes? ❏ Yes ❏ No			
Are the changes effective? That is, is the process showing improvement? Explain:			
Objective evidence: (What was sampled?)		Objective evidence: Customer-specific requirements applicable:	

Figure B.10 Process analysis worksheet.

Appendix C

Confidential Assessment Report for Stage 2

CONTENTS

Organization Information.	114
1. Conduct Audit of Remote Supporting Functions (Recommended).	117
2. Opening Meeting Checklist	119
3. Conduct Facility Tour (Optional)	120
4. Study Customer and Organizational Performance	120
5. Meet with Top Management	120

Organization name:	
City, State:	
Organization contact:	
Lead auditor:	
Audit objectives:	
Audit scope:	
Permitted exclusions:	

Nonconformity	
Total number of nonconformities (issued during audit):	
Major	**Minor**

Figure C.1   Confidential assessment report for stage 2.

6. Audit Organizational Processes 122

 7. Verify That All Processes and Clauses Are Audited 122

 8. Write Up Nonconformities 129

 9. Closing Meeting 131

10. Determine Audit Team Recommendations.................................. 132

11. Prepare the Draft Report... 132

12. Conduct the Closing Meeting 132

13. Audit Report 133

ORGANIZATION INFORMATION

Organization name: _____

Contact person: _____

Department: _____

Telephone: _____

Fax: _____

E-mail: _____

Street: _____

City: _____

State or province: _____

Zip or postal code: _____

Standard: ISO 9001:2015

Type of assessment: Stage 2

Assessment team: _____

Person days: _____

Start date: _____

End date: _____

Assessment information: _____

_____

_____

ASSESSMENT REPORT ACCEPTANCE

Signed for on behalf of auditor:

Name: _____

Date: _____

Signed for on behalf of organization:

Name: _____

Date: _____

AUDIT CONCLUSIONS

Audit Summary: _____

_____

_____

_____

_____

_____

Key issues/concerns requiring top management attention: _____

_____

_____

_____

_____

_____

Opportunities for improvement/observations:			

Previous audit nonconformity status:		
NCRs issued (during last audit):	NCRs closed:	NCRs open:

Changes to organization/facilities/quality management system/scope (since last visit)			
		(as applicable)	
Ref. number	Brief description	Organization document reference	ISO 9001:2015 clause reference

Figure C.2 Opportunities for improvement.

1. CONDUCT AUDIT OF REMOTE SUPPORTING FUNCTIONS (RECOMMENDED)

Site* and/or Remote and/or Support Locations

Please detail individually all sites, including remote locations that support this site (include location name, address, and processes performed that support the site). A support location may be remote to the site or embedded within one site and supporting numerous sites.

Example 1. Site and corporate headquarters located at same location. Corporate headquarters includes human resources, sales, purchasing, and so on, which support other sites.

Example 2. Site A includes a product design center, which supports numerous sites.

Omnex recommends that the site and the supporting functions are audited together in sequence, starting with the supporting functions.

Organization and/or Locations Information Approval Checklist

- Identify processes that link between the support functions and the site. These processes should be evident in the process map. Are they? ❏ Yes ❏ No

- Take samples for each of the processes that will be used to test the interface. Whether these are top management objectives, new products in sales and/or design, or customer satisfaction information provided to the sales office, carefully sample them and follow each process from the supporting function into the site. Does the process link?
❏ Yes ❏ No

- Does the process documentation connect the site to the remote location? ❏ Yes ❏ No

- How is the process managed? Is it working effectively? ❏ Yes ❏ No

- Is it measured, monitored, and improved? ❏ Yes ❏ No

- If the process is not meeting "intended results," is it changed? ❏ Yes ❏ No

- Are the supporting functions and site working together? ❏ Yes ❏ No

- Are they designed to succeed together? ❏ Yes ❏ No

- Is there risk and opportunity analysis and the actions related to processes? ❏ Yes ❏ No

---

*Site refers to the manufacturing location.

Appendix C

Employee Shift Details—Site Remote Support Location

Number	Location name	Market/customers	Street	City	Postal code/ZIP	Postal code/ZIP	Already assessed to ISO 9001:2015

Figure C.3 Employee shift details—site/remote/support location.

2. OPENING MEETING CHECKLIST

❏ Introduce audit team and attendees

❏ Pass out the attendance sheet

❏ Explain the risk and process approach

❏ Review objectives, scope, and criteria

❏ Review supporting functions and interfacing processes

❏ Summary of methods and procedures used for audit:

   ❏ Auditor takes notes of details for both conformities and nonconformities

   ❏ Audit conclusion is based on samples taken

   ❏ The audit will include a cross-section of the organization, from top management to maintenance workers and engineers

   ❏ The audit is restricted to small groups of three or fewer people

   ❏ The auditor notifies the auditee of nonconformities during the audit as well as during a daily review meeting

   ❏ Questions should be directed toward the lead auditor

   ❏ Conditions for when a major nonconformity affecting the customer is uncovered.

❏ Establish auditee communication link

❏ Reconfirm the following:

   ❏ Current customers and interested parties

   ❏ Customer satisfaction and complaint status, including customer reports and scorecards

   ❏ Any customer special status (bad supplier status)

   ❏ Supporting functions and interfacing processes

❏ Review prioritized audit plan

❏ Confirm status of stage 1 issues, including documentation

❏ Confirm time and date of closing meeting

❏ Confirm relevant safety, emergency, and security procedures

3. CONDUCT FACILITY TOUR (OPTIONAL)

- Modify the audit plan based on information collected during the opening meeting and facility tour.

- Note on the Process Analysis Worksheets issues or areas to investigate.

4. STUDY CUSTOMER AND ORGANIZATIONAL PERFORMANCE

- Note: This step is especially important if there is a large time period between the stage 1 and stage 2 audits.

- Reexamine the customer scorecard. Has performance maintained the same level, or has performance deteriorated since the stage 1 audit?

- Study the last business performance review. Has performance sustained at the same level? Did the organization act and follow up on the actions identified from the management review provided during the readiness review?

- Has the organization been put on a special status notification?

- Determine whether to adjust or reprioritize the audit plan based on the latest customer and performance issues.

5. MEET WITH TOP MANAGEMENT

The meeting with top management includes a number of obligations from ISO 9001:2015 clause 5.0, Leadership, and clause 9.3, Management Review.

Auditor Requirements

As discussed earlier, top management's responsibilities are key to a successful quality management system (QMS) implementation. Moreover, ISO 9001:2015 has specific requirements for top management to fulfill. This audit of top management should take place within the context of the processes in the PEI audit trail.

Interview top management to learn the following:

- Alignment of the context, interested party expectations, quality policy, objectives, and *compatibility* with the strategic direction of the organization.

- *Integration* of the QMS with the business processes. In other words, there is only one set of processes running the organization.

- Understanding and *promotion* of risk-based thinking and the process approach.

- What the QMS *intended results* are and whether the organization is meeting them.

- Understanding of customer expectations and customer satisfaction and steps taken to improve customer satisfaction.

- Involvement in establishing, implementing, and maintaining the quality policy.

- Understanding of customer and regulatory requirements and whether the organization is in compliance (*consistently met*). How do they track the requirements? What is the process for understanding and meeting them?

- Whether top management is taking ownership of the effectiveness of the management system. Whether they are taking an active role in working with subordinates (*engaging, directing and supporting*) and/or others in ensuring *effectiveness*.

- *Supporting* other managers in performing their responsibilities, that is, *demonstration* of leadership.

- Review of the quality management system at a periodic frequency to assess the "*suitability, adequacy, effectiveness, and alignment*" with the organization's overall "*strategic direction.*"

- Role in assigning specific roles and responsibilities as required (see clause 5.3).

The points above directly relate to clause 5.0, Leadership, and clause 9.3, Management Review. Not understanding what the standard means and/or top management delegating responsibilities to others could very well result in a nonconformance for top management.

Overall, do the interactions with top management show a good understanding of the QMS and its performance? Is top management "accountable" to the effectiveness of the QMS?

Management Responsibilities That Can Be Delegated

Certain top management activities can be delegated, and some can't. When the word "ensure" is used in ISO 9001:2015, as in clause 5.1, Leadership and Commitment, those items can be delegated.

After the interview, how well did the top manager answer the relevant questions asked regarding the QMS and its performance, alignment of the QMS with strategic direction, process performance, customer satisfaction, and risk-based thinking? Is top management playing their part for the success of the QMS and supporting their subordinates to ensure overall success of the QMS?

The auditor is asked to document his or her observations and record them.

6. AUDIT ORGANIZATIONAL PROCESSES

- Demonstrate the use of the Process Analysis Worksheet and leadership, including the prioritized audit plan.

- Use the stage 2 audit report, Process Analysis Worksheet, and ISO 9001:2015 conformance checklist (see Appendix D) as primary tools for auditing processes.

- Use the audit plan and the organization's defined processes, including sequence and interaction. Don't be requirements oriented; be process oriented.

- Be able to determine whether the organization is operating according to its process definition (that is, a process map and its sequence and interactions. See Chapter 3 and Appendix A). Do the processes reflect reality?

- Audit processes to determine whether each one is capable of meeting the process indicators and is performing satisfactorily.

- Make sure that the customer-specific quality management system requirements are identified, addressed, and maintained in the QMS. (Note: Customer-specific requirements should be integrated into the processes.)

- Conduct interviews about the process with those who are involved in the process at its location. Avoid conference room audits. Always take samples or have the auditees show objective evidence when interviewing them to confirm their statements. The auditor should always choose the samples to avoid biased samples being given.

- Document both conformity and nonconformity in the Process Analysis Worksheet. The information should be clear enough for an independent review by a third party, if necessary.

- Use the Risk Sampling Sheet (Figure C.4) and Quality Objectives Sampling Sheet (Figure C.5) to assess context, interested party expectations, and risk. Note: These sheets were started in stage 1, and insights and evidence gathered in stage 1 can be utilized in stage 2.

In Figure C.5, the same quality objectives as above are reviewed for their plan, how they are deployed within the organization, and whether the management review shows evidence that the objectives are being met.

7. VERIFY THAT ALL PROCESSES AND CLAUSES ARE AUDITED

The auditor should follow the audit plan and ensure that the audit encompassed all processes and clauses. Complete the stage 2 Documentation and Process Cross-Reference (Figure C.6).

Risk Sampling Sheet					
Related interested party expectations* and internal/external issues (4.1 and 4.2)	Objectives and/or intended results (6.1.1)	Related risk and opportunities (6.1.1)	Plan to address risk and opportunities (6.1.2)	Related processes (6.1.2)	Evidence of actions implemented and effectiveness tracked (9.3.2)

*Note: Which internal and external issues and expectations are key to the organization? Has the organization adequately handled these expectations and issues when they set the objectives or "intended results"?

Figure C.4 Risk sampling sheet.

Quality Objectives Sampling Sheet			
Quality objectives	Plan for meeting objectives (what will be done, resources, who is responsible, when it will be completed, how results will be evaluated) (6.2.1)	Deployed objectives (sample department and identify deployed objectives)	Objective evidence of objectives being met and actions completed (9.3.2)

*Quality objectives relate to the needs and expectations of interested parties and could result in objectives related to product quality, on-time delivery, or other expectations critical to an interested party, including customers. Note: Clause 6.2.1 requires quality objectives to be consistent with quality policy, be measurable, satisfy requirements, be relevant to products/services and customer satisfaction, and be monitored, communicated, and updated.

Figure C.5 Quality objectives sampling sheet.

Documentation and Process Cross-Reference for ISO 9001:2015				
Clause	Clause heading	Organization's process number/description/ document reference[1,2]	Process owner[1]	Stage 1 result[3] (C-O-N/A)
4	Context of the organization			
4.1	Understanding the organization and its context			
4.2	Understanding the needs and expectations of interested parties			
4.3	Determining the scope of the quality management system			
4.4	Quality management system and its processes			
4.4.1	No Title			
4.4.2	No Title			
5	Leadership			
5.1	Leadership and commitment			
5.1.1	General			
5.1.2	Customer focus			
5.2	Policy			
5.2.1	Establishing the quality policy			
5.2.2	Communicating the quality policy			
5.3	Organizational roles, responsibilities and authorities			
6	Planning			
6.1	Actions to address risks and opportunities			
6.1.1	No Title			
6.1.2	No Title			
6.2	Quality objectives and planning to achieve them			
6.2.1	No Title			
6.2.2	No Title			
6.3	Planning of changes			
7	Support			
7.1	Resources			
7.1.1	General			
7.1.2	People			
7.1.3	Infrastructure			
7.1.4	Environment for the operation of processes			
7.1.5	Monitoring and measuring resources			
7.1.5.1	General			
7.1.5.2	Measurement traceability			
7.1.6	Organizational knowledge			
7.2	Competence			
7.3	Awareness			
7.4	Communication			
7.5	Documented information			

Figure C.6 Documentation and process cross-reference for ISO 9001:2015.

| Documentation and Process Cross-Reference for ISO 9001:2015 |||||
Clause	Clause heading	Organization's process number/description/ document reference[1,2]	Process owner[1]	Stage 1 result[3] (C-O-N/A)
7.5.1	General			
7.5.2	Creating and updating			
7.5.3	Control of documented information			
7.5.3.1	No title			
7.5.3.2	No title			
8	Operation			
8.1	Operational planning and control			
8.2	Requirements for products and services			
8.2.1	Customer communication			
8.2.2	Determining the requirements for products and services			
8.2.3	Review of the requirements for products and services			
8.2.3.1	No title			
8.2.3.2	No title			
8.2.4	Changes to requirements for products and services			
8.3	Design and development of products and services			
8.3.1	General			
8.3.2	Design and development planning			
8.3.3	Design and development inputs			
8.3.4	Design and development controls			
8.3.5	Design and development outputs			
8.3.6	Design and development changes			
8.4	Control of externally provided processes, products and services			
8.4.1	General			
8.4.2	Type and extent of control			
8.4.3	Information for external providers			
8.5	Production and service provision			
8.5.1	Control of production and service provision			
8.5.2	Identification and traceability			
8.5.3	Property belonging to customers or external providers			
8.5.4	Preservation			
8.5.5	Post-delivery activities			
8.5.6	Control of changes			
8.6	Release of products and services			
8.7	Control of nonconforming outputs			
8.7.1	No title			
8.7.2	No title			
9	Performance evaluation			

Figure C.6 *Continued.*

\multicolumn{5}{c}{Documentation and Process Cross-Reference for ISO 9001:2015}
Clause	Clause heading	Organization's process number/description/ document reference[1,2]	Process owner[1]	Stage 1 result[3] (C-O-N/A)
9.1.1	General			
9.1.2	Customer satisfaction			
9.1.3	Analysis and evaluation			
9.2	Internal audit			
9.2.1	No title			
9.2.2	No title			
9.3	Management review			
9.3.1	General			
9.3.2	Management review inputs			
9.3.3	Management review outputs			
10	Improvement			
10.1	General			
10.2	Nonconformity and corrective action			
10.2.1	No title			
10.2.2	No title			
10.3	Continual improvement			

Note 1: Shaded areas in light gray are to be completed by the organization (auditee); areas in the darker gray are to be completed by the auditor.

Note 2: Process numbers/descriptions/document references must be linked to the organization's (auditee's) process map.

Note 3: C refers to "conformance," O refers to "observations," and N/A stands for "not applicable."

C is in conformance for all documented processes if all the "shalls" are addressed in the documentation. Also, the processes need to include "who," "what," and "when."

Figure C.6 *Continued.*

Stage 2 Audit Plan					
Objective: To verify conformance to ISO 9001:2015					
Date	Time	Auditor	Location	Organization's process # and/or description	Standard clauses

Figure C.7 Stage 2 audit plan.

Process Analysis Worksheet

Company name:	Location:	Audit type:	Standard:
Auditor name:		Process:	
Reponsibilities/Process owner (clause 4.4.1e)		Process linkages (Predecessor) Subsequent process (clause 4.4.1b)	

Applicable clauses:

Related quality objective or QMS performance metric:

What? (Materials/equipment)
Who? (Competence/skills/training)
Inputs → PROCESS → Outputs
How? (Methods/procedures/techniques)
Criteria (Measurement/assessment)

Related risk and opportunities analysis: ❏ Yes ❏ Not applicable

Are the actions implemented? ❏ Yes ❏ No Explain:

Is the organization meeting process performance indicators? ❏ Yes ❏ No

If no, are there planned changes? ❏ Yes ❏ No

Are the changes effective? That is, is the process showing improvement? Explain:

Objective evidence:	Objective evidence:
(What was sampled?)	Customer-specific requirements applicable:

Figure C.8 Process analysis worksheet.

8. WRITE UP NONCONFORMITIES

Please respond by using your own corrective action method (for example, 7D, 8D, or five whys) in the same way that your organization would respond to a customer issue. Include the root cause analysis and systemic corrective action; failure to include these will result in your responses being rejected by the lead auditor.

Writing Nonconformities

- A written nonconformity must contain a statement of nonconformity with the system, the unmet standard requirement, and objective evidence. Note: One nonconformity can be written to cover more than one "shall."

- Categorize nonconformities as major or minor.

- Nonconformities should be cross-referenced to the organization's quality management system (QMS) and/or relevant clause of ISO 9001:2015.

- Identify opportunities for recommendations without offering solutions.

- Use a format that includes root cause, corrective action, and systemic action.

Opportunity for Improvement

Opportunities for improvement (OFI) don't require a formal response but may be revisited at future assessments.

	Corrective Action Request			F17-3
				Revision B
Part A	**Audit information**			
Department		Audit number		
Activity audited		CAR number		
Auditor		Date issued		
Auditee		Reference		
Part B	**Nonconformity**			

Nonconformity:

Requirement:

Objective evidence:

Auditor　　　　　　　　　　Date　　　　　Department representative　　　　Date

Part C	**Corrective/preventive action**

Immediate action:　　　　　　　　　　　　　　Preventive action:

Root cause:

Corrective action:

Auditor　　　　　　　　　　Date　　　　　Department representative　　　　Date

Part D	**Verification of corrective action**

Follow-up details:

Auditor　　　　　　　　　　Date　　　　　Department representative　　　　Date

Figure C.9　Corrective action request.

Nonconformity number	Location and process	Clause	Status (that is, major or minor)	Nonconformity

Note: Each nonconformity must include the standard requirement, objective evidence, and nonconformity.

Figure C.10 Nonconformity chart.

9. CLOSING MEETING

The auditor is responsible for three things during step 9, the closing meeting:

- Determine audit team recommendations
- Prepare draft report
- Conduct closing meeting

10. DETERMINE AUDIT TEAM RECOMMENDATIONS

Once all of the nonconformities are written, step 10 focuses on the audit team's recommendations. There are four outcomes:

- Minor and major nonconformities are so numerous that another readiness review and stage 2 on-site audit are required.
- Minor nonconformities that can be closed via written documentation.
- Minor nonconformities that require on-site closeout.
- Major nonconformities that require on-site closeout.

11. PREPARE THE DRAFT REPORT

- Prepare draft reports describing all nonconformities. Also, identify and include the audit team summary, at a minimum.
- Identify nonconformities and opportunities for improvement. No other categories are allowed.

12. CONDUCT THE CLOSING MEETING

A typical closing meeting agenda includes the following:

- Statement of thanks
- Attendance list
- Scope, objectives, and criteria
- Significance of audit samples
- Audit standard, rules, and reference manuals
- Audit summary
- Nonconformity statements, root cause, and systemic corrective action responses
- Opportunities for improvement
- Clarification of nonconformity statements and summary
- Statement of confidentiality
- Follow-up
- Close

13. AUDIT REPORT

A statement and summary are required in the audit report.

1. Alignment of context, interested party expectations, objectives, processes, risk-based actions (clause 6.2.2), and quality objective actions (clause 6.2.2). Is there alignment? (Yes or No) _____

   Is the action implemented effective on risk and opportunity analysis? (Yes or No)

2. Is top management showing Leadership and "accountability" for "intended results"? (Yes or No) _____

3. Is the management system effective in achieving intended results and customer satisfaction? (Yes or No) _____

4. Management review results and actions: _____

5. Is there progress toward continual improvement? (Yes or No) _____

6. Are internal audit results and corrective actions completed for a full system audit? (Yes or No) _____

7. Are customer complaints decreasing, and is corrective action effective? (Yes or No)

   _____
   _____
   _____

8. Documented information structure and revision status: _____

   _____
   _____
   _____

   Include document changes since the last assessment.

Appendix D

ISO 9001:2015 Conformance Checklist

Note: Due to copyright issues, the ISO 9001:2015 conformance checklist is not included in its entirety.

ISO 9001:2015 Conformance Checklist

Clause number	Requirements	What to audit	Notes and objective evidence	Stage 1 (Y/N)	Stage 2 (Y/N)
4	**Context of the organization**				
4.1	**Understanding the organization and its context**				
	The organization shall determine external and internal issues that are relevant to its purpose and its strategic direction and that affect its ability to achieve the intended result(s) of its quality management system.				
	The organization shall monitor and review information about these external and internal issues.				
	Note 1: Issues can include positive and negative factors or conditions for consideration.				
	Note 2: Understanding the external context can be facilitated by considering issues arising from legal, technological, competitive, market, cultural, social, and economic environments, whether international, national, regional, or local.				
	Note 3: Understanding the internal context can be facilitated by considering issues related to values, culture, knowledge and performance of the organization.				
4.2	**Understanding the needs and expectations of interested parties**				
	Due to their effect or potential effect on the organization's ability to consistently provide products and services that meet customer and applicable statutory and regulatory requirements, the organization shall determine:				
	a. The interested parties that are relevant to the quality management system				
	b. The requirements of these interested parties that are relevant to the quality management system				
	The organization shall monitor and review information about these interested parties and their relevant requirements.				

Effective:
Revision:

Figure D.1 ISO 9001:2015 conformance checklist.
©2015 Omnex, Inc.

Index

A

audit
    follow-up, 80–81
    internal, evaluating, 46–47
    on-site, 57–81
    opening meeting, 59–60
    postponement of, reasons for, 54
    of remote supporting functions, 59
    stage 1, 17–18
    stage 2, 18–22
    system, evaluating, 47
audit feasibility, 53–54
audit plan
    creating, 51–53
    following, 63
    in stage 1 audit, 35
audit planning, and audit trails, 62–63
audit procedure, 57–81
audit report
    stage 1, 55
    stage 2, 74–76
audit responsibilities, determining, 87–88
audit results, determining, 87–88
audit trails, 18–22
    and audit planning, 62–63
    ISO 9001:2015 audit approach, 22–31
auditing strategy, for ISO 9001:2015, 17–34

B

business context, in ISO 9001:2015, 1

C

clause (elemental) approach, versus process approach, 47
closing meeting, 73
    conducting, 74
conformance auditing, versus performance auditing, xiii, 17
context, in ISO 9001:2015, 6
corporate responsibility, xiv
corrective action
    and closeouts, 76–78
    formats used in industry, 78–79
    sample, 79–80
    system, versus incident-specific, 78
    systemic, evaluating, 78–80
customer complaints, 46
customer satisfaction, 71
    and intended results, 46
    performance, studying, 67
customer scorecards, 44–45

D

design failure mode and effects analysis (DFMEA), 10
document review, in stage 1 audit, 17–18, 35
documented information review, in stage 1 audit, 17–18, 35, 36–37, 41–43
draft audit report, preparing, 73

E

elemental (clause) approach, versus process approach, 47
"ensure," under ISO 9001:2015, 68

F

facility tour, conducting, 64–67
failure mode and effects analysis (FMEA), 10

feasibility review, in stage 1 audit, 35
first-article inspection (FAI), 27, 28
follow-up audit, 80–81

H

high level structure (HLS), in ISO 9001:2015 standard, 1, 12–14

I

integrated management systems, xiv
intended results, and customer satisfaction, 46
interested party expectations, 71
    in ISO 9001:2015, 7
internal audit, evaluating, 46–47
ISO 9001 standards
    evolution of, xiii–xiv
    history of, 1–2
ISO 9001:2015 standard, 1
    Annex A, changes from ISO 9001:2008, 16
    audit trails in, 18–22, 22–31
    auditing strategy for, 17–34
    changes from ISO 9001:2008, 14–16
    conformance checklist (Appendix D), 135–36
    high level structure (HLS) in, 1, 12–14
    introduction to, 1–16
    process focus in, 4–6
    requirements for risk, 9–10
    risk in, 3–4
    risk-based thinking, requirement for, 10–11
    use of risk and opportunities in, 8–9, 10–11
ISO 9001:1987 standard, 1
ISO 9001:2000 standard, 1
ISO 14001 standard, 2
    definition of risk under, 7–8
ISO 19011:2011 standard, auditing requirements, 57
ISO 31000:2009 standard, definition of risk under, 7–8
ISO Joint Technical Coordination Group (JTCG), 12
ISO Technical Board, 12

K

key indicators, 50
    measuring, 49–50
Khanna, Tarun, 6

L

leadership audit trail, 20, 25–26
logistics FMEA, 10

M

major nonconformity, 71
management
    responsibilities that can be delegated, 68
    top, meeting with, 67–68
management review, of QMS, 47–49
minor nonconformity, 71–72

N

new product development (NPD) audit trail, 20, 26–28
nonconformities
    requirements for, 72
    sample, 79–80
    writing up, 69–73

O

OHSAS 18001 standard, 2
on-site audit, 57–81
    conducting, 57–81
organizational charts, 87–88
organizational processes, auditing, 68–69
overall performance, versus process performance, 87

P

performance analysis, in stage 1 audit, 35, 44–51
performance auditing, versus conformance auditing, xiii, 17
performance trends, 49–50
performance-based audit trail, 22, 30
plan–do–check–act (PDCA) cycle, 9
    in ISO 9001:2015, 2–3, 13
planning, and risk and opportunities, 7–9
planning, performance evaluation, and improvement audit trail, 19, 24–25, 47
postponement of audit, reasons for, 54
problem solving, performance, 46
process analysis worksheet, 31, 35, 55, 63–64
    completing, 31–34
process approach, xiii, 37
    versus clause (elemental) approach, 47
process characteristics, essential, 83–85
process documentation, 42–43
process failure mode and effects analysis (PFMEA), 10
process focus
    auditing, 87–89
    introduction to (Appendix A), 83–89
    in ISO 9001:2015, 4–6
    studying, 89

process interfaces
    between site and support function, 85–86
    studying, 39–40
process links, studying, 39–40
process map, 37–39
    clause (elemental) based, 39–40
    functional, 39–41, 89
    and process interfaces, 86
    understanding, 83
process performance, 31
    versus overall performance, 87
process performance audit, conducting, 31–34
processes
    measuring and monitoring, 86–87
    organizational, auditing, 68–69
    sequence and interaction of, 37–39, 88
    suspect, identifying, 50–51
    understanding, 83
product and process risk and opportunities, 9–10
production and service provision audit trail, 21, 28–29
production part approval process (PPAP), 27, 28

Q

quality
    definition, 2
    evolution of, xiii–xiv
quality management, definition, 2
quality management system (QMS), 2–4
    context, 7
    model, 2–3
    performance, 31, 47–49
    processes and planning, 9
    processes and planning risk, 9
    processes of, 3–4
    structure, 2–3
quality objectives sampling sheet, 25
quality policy, 2

R

relevancy, in sampling, 62
remote supporting functions, audit of, 59

representative sampling, 62–63
results, intended, and customer satisfaction, 46
risk, 12
    definition, 7
    in ISO 9001 standard, xiv
    in ISO 9001:2015 standard, 1
    requirements for, under ISO 9001:2015, 9–10
    understanding, 7–8
risk and opportunity audit trail, 18–19, 22–24, 47
risk sampling sheet, 23
risk-based thinking, 11, 12
    ISO 9001:2015 requirements for, 10–11
risks and opportunities, 4
    and planning, 7–9
    product and process, 9–10
    use in ISO 9001:2015, 8–9
root cause analysis, evaluating, 78–80

S

sampling, 27, 29, 62–63
scope of audit, 28, 62, 87
scorecards, customer, 44–45
sequence and interaction of processes, 37–39, 88
"shall," under ISO 9001:2015, 42
stage 1 audit, 17–18
    assessment report for (Appendix B), 91–111
    conducting, under ISO 9001:2015, 35–54
stage 2 audit, 18–22
    conducting, 57–81
    confidential assessment report for (Appendix C), 113–34
    flow diagram, *58*
    steps, 57–58
support process audit trail, 20–21, 29–30
suspect processes, identifying, 50–51
sustainability, xiv
system audit
    evaluating, 47
    results, 46–47

T

turtle diagram, 31, 34, 63

The Knowledge Center
www.asq.org/knowledge-center

Learn about quality. Apply it. Share it.

ASQ's online Knowledge Center is the place to:

- Stay on top of the latest in quality with Editor's Picks and Hot Topics.
- Search ASQ's collection of articles, books, tools, training, and more.
- Connect with ASQ staff for personalized help hunting down the knowledge you need, the networking opportunities that will keep your career and organization moving forward, and the publishing opportunities that are the best fit for you.

Use the Knowledge Center Search to quickly sort through hundreds of books, articles, and other software-related publications.

www.asq.org/knowledge-center

TRAINING   CERTIFICATION   CONFERENCES   MEMBERSHIP   **PUBLICATIONS**

Ask a Librarian

Did you know?

- The ASQ Quality Information Center contains a wealth of knowledge and information available to ASQ members and non-members

- A librarian is available to answer research requests using ASQ's ever-expanding library of relevant, credible quality resources, including journals, conference proceedings, case studies and Quality Press publications

- ASQ members receive free internal information searches and reduced rates for article purchases

- You can also contact the Quality Information Center to request permission to reuse or reprint ASQ copyrighted material, including journal articles and book excerpts

- For more information or to submit a question, visit **http://asq.org/knowledge-center/ask-a-librarian-index**

Visit **www.asq.org/qic for more information.**

TRAINING　　CERTIFICATION　　CONFERENCES　　MEMBERSHIP　　**PUBLICATIONS**